DEVASTATION SONGS:
AN ANTHOLOGY OF KAIJU WRITING

Alex Adams is a writer and musician based in North East England. They have published four critical books on political violence in popular culture, and they are writing *Godzilla: A Critical Demonology*, which will be a full critical account of every Godzilla film. For full information on their writing and music, visit atadamswriting.com. They can be found on social media at @gdemonology and @AlexAdams5

Aaron Kent is a working-class writer, stroke survivor, and insomniac from Cornwall. His 2nd collection, *The Working Classic*, is available from the87press. He has read his poetry for The BBC, The Shakespeare Birthplace Trust, and Stroke Association, had work published in various journals, and is an Arvon tutor. His poetry has been translated into languages including French, Hungarian, German, Cymraeg, and Kernewek, and has been set to music.

ISBN: 978-1-916938-57-1

Cover designed by Aaron Kent

Cover image: © rosi_a / Adobe Stock

Edited by: Alex Adams & Aaron Kent

Typeset by Aaron Kent

Broken Sleep Books Ltd
PO BOX 102
Llandysul
SA44 9BG

Devastation Songs:
an anthology of kaiju writing

Edited by
Alex Adams & Aaron Kent

Broken Sleep Books

CONTENTS

Our fascination with giant monsters is as ancient and ingrained as our love of literature itself. One of the earliest texts of what we now call science fiction is Margaret Cavendish's Hollow Earth novel *The Blazing World*, published in 1666, and it overflows with baroque specimens of cryptozoology; legendary monsters, of course, such as Beowulf's Grendel, Japanese *Yokai*, or the Titans of Greek myth, predate writing itself. The modern Kaiju genre which inherits these traditions is as healthy as it has ever been, and it continues to inspire new adherents with its grand visions of apocalyptic destruction and wrestlemania pugilism. It is notable, after all, that two of the original creatures that birthed the giant monster movie – Godzilla and King Kong – retain their blockbusting iconic status, having returned to cinema screens in one of 2024's biggest and most popular movies, *Godzilla x Kong: The New Empire*.

Occupying its own distinct niche in the messy overlap between spectacle cinema, horror, sci-fi, fantasy, action, and children's entertainment, perhaps the kaiju movie is so popular and enduring a form because it is able to appeal to our primeval fascination with monstrosity at the same time as it engages with so many powerfully resonant social and political ideas. After all, the genre is often most celebrated when it has something to say with its terrifying voice. *Godzilla Minus One* is a harrowing exploration of post-war recovery and private guilt. *Godzilla 1984* is a Cold War fable about the fragility of peace and the looming danger of mutually assured thermonuclear destruction. *Shin Godzilla* is a satire of the bumbling Japanese gerontocracy whose ineptitude and corruption so worsened the 2011 Fukushima disaster. (These more serious concerns have informed our decision to donate the proceeds of this volume to Freedom From Torture, an organisation that works with torture survivors, refugees, and displaced people fleeing war and disaster.) Nobody, however, would claim that attending to the political messaging in some of the better known movies fully explains why so many of us love kaiju flicks so fervently. It's the fact that these films *say these things with monsters* that really makes them so attractive. *Godzilla Vs Biollante*, for instance, is a film about global resource wars and the biotech arms race; but it's also a labyrinthine, gothic story, featuring a supremely eldritch monster composed of plant matter, Godzilla's own DNA, and the soul of a dead teenager. So much of the attraction of the genre is the appeal of the strange, the wondrous, and the mysterious. There's high seriousness, yes, but there's also simply awe: the wriggling, bloodthirsty void which eludes or resists explanation. And, what's more, sometimes giant creatures punch each other in the face.

Speaking for myself, I first developed a love of monster movies when I encountered late-night screenings of Toho's Showa classics. In the mid-nineties, Channel Four showed a run of old-school favourites in the run-up to Roland Emmerich's 1998 Hollywood Godzilla movie, and without quite knowing what I was watching I gobbled up *Son of Godzilla*, *Terror of Mechagodzilla*, *Destroy All Monsters*, and more. Like many upon my first encounter with these movies, my amazement and delight mingled with bafflement and perplexity. Utterly ill-equipped to understand the films, knowing nothing about the directors and stars whose names I would later memorise, I was nonetheless immediately hooked at a tender age by their singular audacity, their vertiginous oscillation between deathly seriousness and gleeful silliness, and the sheen of glamour they acquired by being broadcast at such a late, forbidden hour. Rediscovering the movies later in life, I found that this charm had changed but by no means disappeared. As an adult I still enjoy tracking down the many movies that were, in my pre-internet youth, simply impossible to learn about, let alone acquire, and they continue to thrill me with their bizarre, luminous instantiations of impossible worlds. There's something of this wonder, too, in the poems and stories that Aaron and I have collected here in this volume. From stanza to stanza, line to line, the bonkers beauty of the genre overflows from these gorgeous, mesmerizing slices of imagination. Like Kaiju, these pieces speak of the bizarre, the beyond, and, ultimately, of the human.

— Alex Adams

On the plane home from my first trip abroad in 8 years, I sat with my daughter as my wife sat next to our son. Our children had never been on a plane before but found the whole experience delightful. As Rue focused on her colouring book, Otis snacked on monkey shaped crisps, and Emma read her kindle I watched *Godzilla Minus One* on my phone. 45 minutes from the end of the film I noticed Rue had begun to watch it with me, and so the questions began. *Why are they trying to hurt Godzilla? IS Godzilla real? Is Godzilla a goodie or a baddie?* And so began my opportunity to talk to a captive audience about giant monsters.

As the film rolled towards its end and (spoilers ahead) Godzilla inevitably met his fate with an abundance of weaponry, my daughter felt the same response I did upon watching kaiju films as a kid, a deep sadness at the fate of the 'monster'. However, something struck me about this film as different, something that I hadn't seen in kaiju films before. The humans who caused Godzilla's demise saluted him as he went down, paying their respects as an acknowledgement that, as Chon A. Noriega writes in *Godzilla and the Japanese Nightmare: When Them! Is U.S.*, 'The monster created by the bomb requires the bomb to kill the monster. This is the circuitous logic of the arms race.'

And so it goes, humanity creates the things it suggests will save itself, only to destroy those things that endanger it with new things it will present as necessary. Kaiju films present this warped logic in a way that can pull at the heartstrings of a six-year-old girl on a plane, and her thirty-five-year-old father, and does so while with all of the abundance cinema can offer. There aren't many art forms that so deftly weave the human condition with art so flawlessly, and here, in this book, I hope we have emulated that.

— Aaron Kent

THIRTEEN WAYS OF LOOKING AT A KAIJU

I
Sprouts of feverfew
From Nagasaki dust
Blurts Rodan.

II
Mothra spends two hundred million years
A worm,
Sunning underground,
And one day
As a butterfly.

III
Isle huff and
Isle puff
And I'll blow your metropolis
Into particles
Whose particles will penetrate
In2   and
            cells
Part(into other)icles.

IV
Ebirah wakes
On the wrong side
Of the Great Pacific Garbage Patch,
Is scuttling along the floors
Of silent seas this morning

Surceasing all he sees
Beneath the seas—
The ragged scene descends.
The clause ends.

V

To defeat Astro-Monster
Use the Lady Guard Alarm
To Mars Attacks these double X-ers;
All the medicine in the world
Cannot cure an Earth
Without Godzilla.

VI

Buckets of sand
Make their way from the deserts
To finish *The Conqueror*.
By the time Godzilla's on ice,
You are already defeated.

VII

The Lucky Dragon's crew
Saw two suns in the sky
They cried
When their skin began to bubble
In the snow.
Bravo. Encore. Encore. Encore.
When your son hatches,
Snow won't fall
Unless we tell it to.
(Keep us abreast).

VIII

A photocopier and a rat's nest
Made of phonelines
Are tangled in the boardroom.
Shin Godzilla
Stands at attention,
His destruction imminent
Awaiting a motion, a second, and approval.

IX

Is it better to be a woman
Turned into a monster?
Or a monster
Turned into a woman?
Uptown or downtown
They'll crucify you.
Stay off the Brooklyn Bridge.

X

The twins of Infant Island
Are not as small as they look;
Their voices carry
For millenia.

XI

This just in:
White American reporter
Visits friend from college
In Japan. Lean in.
Did this friendship blossom
Before or

after the internment camps?
A no-no boy's return?
A graduate of Imaginary University?
No. No. Not that.

XII

Our *kaiju* who art in heaven
Ghidora be thy name
Thy will be done
On Venus as it is in heaven.
I pledge allegiance,
To Ghidora of the United States of America,
And to the republic for which he lands,
One kaiju, under kaiju,
With liberty and terror for all.
Kaiju the hour is getting late.
It's almost time to hibernate.

XIII

Spools of silver nitrate
(Mothra's web)
Spin around the equator
As it blisters, boils, and fizzles.
Get your Nikon Gamera ready.
I know what happens to a dream deferred.
First, they put it in the movies;
Then the projectionist his projector loads
Where
It explodes.

THE EIGHTH CHILD OF THE YAMADA CLAN

If you want a picture of the future, imagine a kaiju foot stamping on a human face—forever.
— Julian Jamie Francis IV

Suzume was off to the university but certainly not to her world mythology lecture. And this quote she found herself obsessing over was from a much more contemporary source—an obscure American writer who'd died a few years prior under mysterious circumstances. When she fixated on these words, she got this feeling that they contained a truth—something inside her—that could not be contained.

Unfortunately, the containment broke first at her lips: she was reciting the words to herself. Suzume hadn't noticed she'd started doing it until a classmate recorded her and uploaded the short clip to The Legion. That social networking site, too, had ways of cracking out of its screened prison and infecting her reality. Soon, people on campus who'd seen the locally viral clip were whispering, calling her 'The Curse Girl' as if she were some horror movie ghoul.

Online bullying was nothing new. But when the entire train car of passengers, overhearing her recitation, turned in uniform to stare swords at Suzume's throat? *This* hostility was new.

The packed Chuo Line shook past Ochanomizu, its passengers rocking in unison. They all looked the same, all eyes locked on Suzume. Since the pandemic, even more people than before wore masks. And now all you saw was their eyes, full of hate. Little puffs of laughter bubbled their cotton masks. To Suzume, it looked as if they were laughing in unison, maybe all at some private joke. Her imagination. Had to be. But she swore they all, in one motion, rubbed their noses through the masks. She knew it might just be a psychological cope, but sometimes she chose to imagine that they were in fact all simply puppets. Remote controlled via The Legion.

Not long after Elon Musk turned Twitter into X, a mysterious Gatsby-esque Japanese financier had pushed The Legion into existence, spending every yen like a man possessed. An 'Everything App' with 'a place for everyone' within its honeycomb logo, The Legion had uniquely addictive features. High on the list were the 'Swarming' topics that even spotlighted individual users to be 'stung' that day for various offenses. Rumor had it that 'Swarms' operated on a top-secret new AI. Others said it was an algorithm that had gained sentience. Sci-fi theories aside, it was true that a handful of teenagers had burst blood vessels in their eyes after days on end staring at The Legion. Rumors—spread on other sites—held that The Legion's CEO himself had paid for their hospital bills and seen not only to their rehabilitation but to happy, gainful employment in the company. A place for everyone—but not Suzume.

Throat growing tight with anxiety, Suzume forced herself to return to her book. Its pages were where she belonged.

***

Suzume Yamada had memorized this Julian Francis quotation— an otaku twist on the classic Orwell line—not because it was particularly clever or well-written. She'd liked Francis's stories well enough (though too many, she thought, hinged on glibly sentimental endings). But it wasn't literary interest that had her mouthing these English words to herself throughout every day like some sutra. It was because, as she read in an interview with the obscure writer on the archive of an equally obscure online literary magazine, Julian Francis had suffered the same repetitive, invasive dream that rampaged through her psyche every night: the famous Disney fawn Bambi, in what looked in her dreams as if it might have been a *sumi-e* ink painting, instantly pulverized under the terrible weight of Godzilla's foot.

Bambi Meets Godzilla was the name of the short, animated film that apparently split this atom of obsession in Francis's mind, though until she tracked down a VHS copy of *Godzilla 1985* in an American memorabilia shop in Umeda, Suzume had never seen the clip itself. Only the reverberation that had entered her dreams.

For a girl who'd had few to no friends, this glimmer of connection—even with a person recently deceased on the other side of the planet—held cryptic significance. When you're the eighth child in your family, a true oddity in Japan, it feels like nothing is yours. How to distinguish yourself? Her eldest siblings Taro and Noriko had children of their own already, company jobs, homes protected by stone walls. Even her oddball just-barely-older brother Junichi had found something, even if it was just a fixation on American culture and an insistence others call him 'Justin.' What parental attention and awareness remained had trickled down to the five that followed, each in early adulthood themselves, so that Suzume's growth and wellness were but the buzz of an insect trapped against a windowpane, aimlessly banging to get to the world. But it seemed there was—or at least had been—one other human being in this world who'd shared a secret with her. This could be her way out of the hive.

***

Since finding out about Julian Francis's dreams and reading his work, she'd been seeking out everything she could find on him. His early literary promise, the onset of his paranoia about impending kaiju domination of the planet, his descent into drink.

One reason she had applied to Sophia was William Curtis, lecturer on contemporary American literature in the Sophia University international school of humanities. He'd been quoted in one small obituary for Francis, remarking that he'd been a dear friend—and that, as best he could, he would carry on 'his mission,' presumably in the world of letters.

'It was a shame what happened to Julian,' Professor Curtis said, leaning back in his office chair. 'You said your name was... Suzume... bachi?'

'Just Suzume.'

'Sorry. Somehow my brain just wanted to tag that 'hornet' on there. Always makes me think of the number eight for some reason. Foreigner Japanese, I guess.'

'If only it were just foreigners,' Suzume said, glancing out the window as she sipped the tea the professor had poured.

'The man always liked to drink,' Professor Curtis said. 'I kept up with him to a point, and then I couldn't. Something just went wrong in his head, and he was like a sink drain, swallowing everything he could. People like that are maybe trying to drown something inside them. In English, we call those 'personal demons,' though even I don't know what his were.'

'So, it was the drinking that did it? I'd read something kind of crazy online that—'

'Look, you don't need to hear the grisly details. It's great that you're enjoying his books, too. So let me just settle this for you: whatever else happened, it was the drink.'

'So, his head remained on his shoulders?'

Professor Curtis rubbed his forehead. He'd clearly explained this—or explained it away—countless times before. The man suddenly looked older, wrinkles setting in like on shriveling fruit in a time lapse video.

'Look, miss Suzume, it's true that he 'lost his head' in a metaphorical sense. He... had some strange ideas as the years and the boozing went on. But that rumor that he was some Yukio Mishima-esque beheaded martyr is just nonsense. And let me stress this: He was a *good man* despite it all. He'd have done anything for his friends. In fact, it was his idea that I even apply to teach here. I'd go so far as to say I'd have died for the guy. Or killed.'

'Well,' she said, mouth smacking dryly, 'I certainly know how rumors can be.'

***

One reason Professor Curtis immediately made space in his schedule for Suzume was that her name was a familiar one. Where her high school faculty and administration had simply chosen to ignore her years of ostracization, the Sophia University higher-ups kept an eye out when the rumors and bullying that had tormented Suzume followed her to their institution. While her obsession with this Julian Jamie Francis character had been a little unusual and her hours holed up in the library reviewing every kaiju film they had on record a little eccentric, the fact that she was at least showing up to class was regarded as a positive sign. Even if she did bring up Julian Francis at least once per class apropos of nothing in the day's lecture.

Still, that didn't prevent the clips of her chiming in during class from being buzzed out on The Legion: #PSYCHOCURSEGIRL. For weeks after that, she got epithet-riddled emails from burner accounts telling her to quit yammering about some nothing foreign author—or better yet, if she couldn't, to slit her own throat and be done with it. In high school, when she still had a profile on The Legion, Suzume would be bombarded throughout the day with vicious comments from anonymous accounts. That default face, a silhouette of a bumblebee, popped up over and over. A hive with no real queen but seemingly one mind that wanted her head. When her brother 'Justin' noticed her bloodshot eyes at his graduation ceremony, he made her promise to get off social media, or he wouldn't leave home. 'Fuck university,' he said. 'Maybe nobody else sees you, but this can't go on.' She rubbed her aching eyes, cried as they hugged goodbye, and deleted her profile while he watched. From then on, her fingers flipped through Justin's old manga and paperback novels instead of algorithmic feeds, and Suzume started to dream of Bambi smooshed by Godzilla feet.

Her absence from The Legion did little to mitigate the way that hive could define her. When her test scores had gotten her into the prestigious Sophia University despite her lacking grades, this only further fueled rumors: bribery, a father involved in the yakuza, sexual favors performed for admissions officers. Hundreds of irate emails per day burst past spam filters. Links to Legion Swarms dunking on her, screenshots of fabricated posts with her name attached. They were transforming her into something they could control. The inconsistency of these accusations and their total lack of evidentiary support did not matter. Like geometrically efficient and mutually supporting hexagonal cells, one flimsy piece of the hive supported the next. And, as Suzume started to believe, the soldier bees would defend the overall structure mindlessly.

On campus, she'd catch people looking her way and wonder which among those buzzing online assholes they were. Every classmate could have been among those trying to crucify her with words—or maybe it wasn't them at all! Suzume didn't know how far the hive went. Only that the volume of hate was incredible. What had she ever done to bring this wave of disdain on herself? Suzume understood she was a little unusual. Her obsessive interests made her appear unsuited for studies, for athletics, for marriage. But it was something simpler than that: Instinct. She was, to the normies, just plain strange. Simply, vaguely, yet uncannily 'creepy.' CREEPY was another of their favorite hashtags.

A species difference. That had to be it, Suzume would sometimes think, detecting this gaze upon her, one mind and a million eyes. Even though we look the same, something inside me is different, and they can sense it. Like a cobra and a mongoose. Or Gamera and Gyaos.

At least, this was how Suzume felt until she discovered Julian Francis's writing and learned she was not the first. There *was* a place for her.

***

'Are you free this evening?' the text message from William Curtis read. Suzume was in her bedroom studying *Terror of Mechagodzilla*, as recently she'd become fixated on mechanical kaiju and the possibility of remote manipulation of both living and bionic beings. That Dr. Mafune from the film, evil from a certain angle, made sense to Suzume. Who wouldn't want to strike back at the society that rejected him?

Suzume assumed Professor Curtis must have gotten her cell number from university records. A minor breach of policy, so something important had to be up. Though she'd already brushed and changed into pajamas, what Professor Curtis had to say pulled her from both kaiju flick and the lure of bed: 'I remembered something about Julian that I think you need to hear.'

***

Suzume never really drank. Even catching a whiff of it on her one friend, a hard-boozing bass player in a local girl band, caused her to recoil slightly. When she got to the izakaya and found William Curtis already thoroughly into his *sake*, she considered simply calling a cab.

'Do you believe,' the drunk professor said, 'in real, living kaiju?'

Professor Curtis insisted he wasn't going to be able to divulge this kaiju secret about Julian Francis until Suzume had caught halfway up to his stupor. *Achilles and the Tortoise*, he said. *To infinity! Though you'll never get there.* Suzume started with draft beer, having learned from the television that this was the traditional starter. Then they moved on to warmed Japanese *sake*, plum wine, and whiskey highballs when Suzume's stomach began to feel overfull from sashimi and booze. The tense atmosphere that had felt like a knife at her throat that afternoon had dissipated. They even discussed their favorite (and 'less accomplished') Julian Francis stories before Suzume got on a tangent about kaiju films and her suspicion that maybe, hear her out, The Legion was pulling society's strings against her. She knew how conspiratorial that sounded, but William Curtis listened attentively so that she kept spilling.

'*Pro-fesh-or*,' she said, pointing her chopsticks at his throat like talons, 'what *exactly* are you aiming to teach me tonight?'

'Well, miss Suzume,' he said, the expression on his face shifting one degree closer to that gravely serious look from his office. 'That belief that there really could be kaiju influencing our world, that was a big part of what drove Julian mad.'

'You mean the Bambi dream?'

'That was the start of the feeling, yes,' he said, pouring a *sake* refill from their carafe. Suzume, hanging on every detail, sipped and munched cabbage dipped in spicy mayonnaise. 'But Julian believed in something genetic. Something about kaiju that could get into people.'

'Like The Legion?'

'Huh? No, not social media. A latent potential, almost like a bloodline.'

Ah, Suzume thought, so this was yet another gag about my family, my eighth-ness.

'Suzume, Julian believed that *he* harbored the genetic potential to *become* a kaiju.'

Professor Curtis signaled their server. 'You kept my good bottle, yes? Let's have that.'

'How does the dream...'

'It wasn't just Julian, though. Suzume, are you familiar with the legend of Yamata no Orochi? Of course, that's hardly the only multi-headed God—or demon—in world stories. Professor Akutami lectured on it, but I suppose you skipped that day. Julian believed the kaiju that would destroy the world had multiple heads—that is, its potential to be reborn lives inside numerous people at any moment throughout history. Can you guess how many?'

Suzume nibbled cabbage and considered what he was getting at. Ghidorah had three heads.

'Bzzzt. Not three, which I know is what a kaiju otaku like you would be thinking. Ah, here we go,' Professor Curtis said as his bottle—apparently kept on hand for a fee—arrived at the table with clean, colorfully glazed stoneware glasses. 'This is the good stuff. Yashiori. Drink up!'

Suzume sipped. Delicious stuff. She held off, seeing that Professor Curtis hadn't touched his cup yet.

'Ah, don't stand on ceremony. I'm still nursing this Suntory,' he said.

Suzume tipped the cup back and found it promptly refilled almost the moment she set it down. Fuck it, she thought. This was my biggest Julian Francis find yet. Just go along with it.

'As it so happens, just like with the Yamata no Orochi legend, Julian's particular delusion involved eight people per generation capable of becoming this humanity-stomping kaiju. What is it with kooks and numerology? Here, let me refill that.'

Suzume had never been so drunk in her life. So euphoric. Even the crazy story Professor Curtis was relaying landed on her as something wonderful—what a wild idea this author had conceived. What did this mean for her special connection with him, then? Their shared dream? Suzume didn't hold any particularly unusual beliefs. Uninterested in politics, mostly indifferent to philosophy. She was just obsessive—and, yes, maybe, if she were pressed on the topic, she may have been a little cynical about the average person. She regretted just a bit disclosing her strange notion about The Legion controlling the world against her. She must have sounded like Julian Francis on his downward slide.

'Suzume,' Professor Curtis said, 'do you hate humanity?'

'Huh?' Suzume felt queasy. The liquor had reached her head, and she couldn't seem to pull the sullen expression off her face. For a moment she thought she might vomit—but no, what was rising wasn't *that*. It did feel like hate. Was it just because Professor Curtis had said that? Was it the booze?

'I know it must have been hard. I hope you won't mind me saying so, but most of the faculty are well aware of the troubles you had prior to Sophia University. And I know some of them have followed you here.'

'I don't know.'

'What I mean is, no one could blame you for hating people, at least a little bit. But it goes beyond that, doesn't it?'

'It's not that. It's... '

'The Legion.'

'Yes!' Suzume said and slapped her cup down harder than she'd meant to. 'I don't hate humanity. But when they all start skittering around together online, just acting like the next one over. To me, they're like *fucking bugs*.'

'There's our hornet girl. The invader that takes a whole hive to take down.'

Suzume felt dizzy. She suddenly wished she were back in her room in her pajamas, '70s kaiju on her screen. *Go! Titanosaurus! Go! Mechagodzilla! Crush the earthlings!*

'It was when Julian felt he couldn't manage that killing feeling anymore that he asked me to do it. Of course, I refused. Did he want to be some kind of American Yukio Mishima? I'd never swung a sword in my life let alone taken off a man's head. Never even been in a real fist fight! But now...'

Suzume's face tingled. Where was her cell phone? She had thought it was resting on the table, but all she could find in the moment was a scattering of empty glasses. William Curtis asked for the bill in Japanese then rubbed his chin, as if arriving at the point of a lecture. He rolled the edge of his glass on the table, like a top winding down to its inevitable fall. Had someone turned down the izakaya's lights?

'There was the Indian kid in Hyderabad—I know, I had to laugh. I love Indian food, but I couldn't eat the whole time until after it was done. We were just lucky it wasn't one of the states that prohibits alcohol.

'Then there was the American girl. Girls and women are harder, you know? Everyone's on guard with alcohol these days, but I can't even feel like some kind of samurai lopping off a helpless woman's head. Even if she is inheritor to a demon spirit. I almost wish Julian were in Hell for leaving me with this shit, but everything goes as he planned. Like I said, this job was his idea. He was sure the final one, the eighth, would turn up in Japan, home of kaiju, origin of Orochi. All we had to do was leave a trail of crumbs and wait for you to come slithering out.

'You know,' William Curtis said, chuckling to himself, and Suzume's limbs were cold, would not answer her internal scream to move, to get away from this lunatic, 'in the story, it's Orochi who had to be filled with powerful liquor before he could be killed.' He hiccupped. His face was flushed like he might cry. And then his face dissolved in Suzume's eyes, like ink on a wet page. 'But every time, it's me who needs to be drunk to go through with this.'

***

From the faint odor of gasoline, the cold concrete floor on her side, and the overhead light, Suzume took her improvised prison to be Professor Curtis's garage. She was bound to a cheap computer chair with rope and tape, gagged, and still partially numb from whatever had been in that Yashiori *sake*. Professor Curtis stood wobbly on whiskey legs, a katana in hand. Standing much more firmly beside him was a man in a ball cap and surgical mask, his own sword still sheathed. Maybe the designated driver and backup decapitator.

'Stand her up,' Professor Curtis said.

'How could you kill Julian?' she said, muffled against the gag. It was like trying to reason with The Legion once they'd labeled her. Feeling was only just started to return to her limbs, but she knew she wouldn't be strong enough to get out of these restraints even if she weren't drugged. 'He was sick. Addicted. And you just fed into his delusion and helped him die?'

'The others tried to lawyer out of it, too,' the masked guy said. 'And then they used whatever meager power they'd manifested already to try to kill us first. We're not so naïve anymore.'

'Be a big girl, Suzume,' Professor Curtis said, 'and smile on your way out like big bro Julian did. You're sparing every human life on earth,' he said, then took a final pull off a bottle of cheap Suntory. 'Not that you'd care.'

Suzume did not smile. She thrashed against the restraints but managed only the weakest wobble. She closed her eyes, tried to brace herself. But then she opened them. The masked man stood at attention, some salaryman playing samurai, doing what William Curtis told him—and Curtis was following Julian Francis's command. Both labored under a delusion—or maybe a belief, true or not—that demanded action. Professor Curtis's eyes were cold and drunk. Not unlike those eyes above surgical masks on the train,

The Legion's social media flickering in reflection. Suzume felt all this rather than thinking through it, and more than a feeling, it was image: the hive. Those perfectly hexagonal shapes interlocking, supporting and controlling the overall shape. Professor Curtis looked like just one more drone, and Suzume was filled with a potent mixture of sympathy and disdain.

Do I hate people?

Revenge on humans was a running theme in kaiju works. The Seatopians sent Megalon to avenge the damage wreaked on home by nuclear tests. Dr. Mafune joined with alien invaders in his quest to punish the academic world that'd rejected him—an extreme but understandable impulse! Godzilla himself has been imagined as all manner of revenge—for nuclear weapons, for the deaths in the Pacific War. Even gentle Mothra was willing to wreak havoc on the innocent as well as the guilty when humanity offended her.

Suzume did not hate all people. Her family—though she'd wished they'd loved her more, loved her as much as they could her elder siblings—were not bad people. 'Justin' showed her kindness, had noticed and tried to protect her. And there was her drunken bassist friend, gone to the world in her own way, who'd buy her curry on the weekend if she came to a show. Even now that she knew Julian Francis had set into motion this plan that would kill her, she couldn't entirely hate him, either. They'd shared a fondness for kaiju—and that dream, of course, innocence crushed under the foot of a monster. Maybe they shared much more. *Smile on your way out like big bro Julian did.* Maybe that was mercy for everyone, for all of humanity locked into the rigid structure of its hive.

What she did hate was how people reminded her so much of mere creatures—and the lowest ones at that. Suzume couldn't be sure if this was an inherent trait or whether it was technology like The Legion creating this in people. But as they were, she regarded them as pests.

When she thought of those uniform faces, uniform eyes trained on the same screens, the same information, the lies and manipulation, she did hate that. The Legion. Yes, she hated that.

She hated The Legion. If this is what humanity's true form was, then yes. She hated them.

Suzume stared as William Curtis raised his katana, batted his eyes against a drunken sleepiness, and swung.

***

Flame spread throughout the garage, feeding on splatters of grease and droplets of fuel, and it ate the bindings that held Suzume's limbs. While the masked man scrambled for an extinguisher and William Curtis reeled, dropping the rapid-heated, glowing hot katana, Suzume slammed the garage opener and stumbled out onto the street.

Flames singed holes in her tee shirt and jeans, but Suzume herself was unharmed—and she felt as if her body had eaten up all the liquor, too. Her skin tingled with pleasure, as if she'd just spent a spa day with the Gods.

Normally, a residential street like this would be virtually dead. Maybe somebody on a bicycle making a convenience store run, a dog-walker. But Suzume found people standing, staring into the light of their phones, humans turned streetlamps. She slowed the pace of her escape, stunned at the number of people, all those glowing beams filling their heads. But these lights weren't there to illuminate her way. This was surveillance. As Suzume marched toward the station, one by one The Legion turned their phones on her, recording, snapping flash photos as she went by.

'What is your problem?' she shouted, covering the parts of her exposed by the burned away clothing. But to Hell with that, she thought, and slapped the phone out of one man's hand.

'*Weir-do*,' he said without the slightest emotional affect. His eyes still reflected the screen glow. There was no mind there anymore.

Suzume grabbed his phone from the ground, and on its cracked screen, she could make out the message he had posted to the world—that they had all posted, reposted, liked, favorited, bookmarked, upvoted, and turned into 'their story.' INTOXICATED SOPHIA

UNIVERSITY STUDENT SEEN LEAVING THE HOME OF AMERICAN PROFESSOR.

So, this was her true, unnatural enemy. And it was using the human species against her, like a technological fungus moving humans like zombie ants against her. Remote control. Dr. Mafune would be proud. Rather than some giant dinosaur, this intelligence—whatever it was—had made the whole of humanity its puppet. Suzume now truly believed this—and she was warming to Julian Fracis's kaiju delusion. For the first time in her life, she was grateful to have been the eighth Yamada child.

Suzume ran. The crowd of phone-lookers, The Legion, staggered in front of her, stalling her progress by mere force of human flesh and bones. She pushed and slapped and wriggled through them until she reached the station.

At the intersection of multiple station hallways, Suzume positioned herself in the middle of the crowd. She felt she needed to be surrounded by humanity to judge it. It didn't take long for all those phone-watchers to circle around. Those simply addicted to dopamine hits kept walking, but those of The Legion lingered, boxing her in, posting her out to the ultimate Legion Swarm Topic. CREEPY GIRL SMELLS OF GASOLINE AT STATION. WHAT'S GOING ON!? #TERROR

Hate finally found Suzume. But so did relief. She understood at last why she had never been able to connect with others. A species difference, indeed. She was at once one of them and always destined to become something else. They could only see it one way, whereas Suzume was quickly learning to see the world from eight points of view. Maybe humans were detestable, but they weren't meant to be bugmen. In the tale, which had come rushing back to Suzume with pristine clarity, Yamata no Orochi had been satisfied with a sacrifice here and there. The Legion wanted them all. *Like Hell I'll allow that.*

After all, she thought, feeling the flames rise and her eight viewpoints sprout and grow looming over the human infestation below. *These are* my *people. And I will show them my mercy.*

LACERTAE DEUS (**TAXONOMY OF WRATH**)

vanguard gulls herald
the king has come to court
as spinal ridges split the sea
prelude to maelstrom landfall

Lepeophtheirus gigantus
slough with water runoff
having found safety
as part of skin cell communion
upon the body of divinity
what must it be like
embraced inside an ecosystem
symbiosed between destruction and rest

the curve of the coast is held in his eyes
are they tired//ancient//last of his kind
do they reflect pain from unintended genesis
are they as indifferent as seasonal hurricanes
or glow pale malice when primates throw spears

cherry blossoms scattered
window pane reverberation
from passing bipedal thunder
apex predators shape ecosystems
apex titans shape worlds
as the tail lays low the landscape

the ruin and restart to modern babel towers
reaches city center as time splits and spills
into light with enough weight to burn
skyscraper metal to sand//sand to glass
it is rage at the gates of lower heaven
as there strides the deathless god atomic

EGG (IMAGINAL DISCS)

There's a scene in *Godzilla Vs Mothra* (1992) where Mothra,
dying,
demolishes the Diet and spins a cocoon,
smothering the corruption of neoliberal politics in her gossamer
        chrysalis.
The caterpillar's last cry –
mournful arcs of silk at sunset
her promise (perhaps her threat) of a coming reincarnation.

During metamorphosis, Lepidoptera
completely dissolve.
While dormant, the larval creature digests itself and becomes
what entomologists call 'tissue cell soup',
a primordial snot
which eventually coalesces into the structure of the new
creature.

So she's in there, churning,
insect slush body,
first grub, then goo, then goddess.
Gestation:
the body is what
the body would be if it was not
the body.

There's Christian iconography in most of the Mothra movies
that complements and amplifies their unambiguous environmentalism
and anticapitalism.

In *Mothra* (1961), for instance, the villain Clark Nelson
is a greasy capitalist plundering the natural world,
(Carl Denham rewritten as malicious twit,
the whimsically charming adventurer revealed as
viciously arrogant slaver, expropriator, colonizer)
and his defeat is enacted underneath a church, the sun's rays
        framing the cross
with a magnificent halo.

So there's this gorgeous connection, in Mothra movies, between
        justice, holiness,
and transformation.
Maybe that's why I love Ando in *Godzilla Vs Mothra* 92:
because, even though he's a bit of a dope,
a labrador salaryman, he is brave enough
to recognize his wrongdoing and change
for the better in the face of injustice.

(Obviously, that's what's good about fantasy films: like parables or
        ballads,
they embarrass you into sincerity – like, of course it's fucking corny,
of course that's Kenpachiro Satsuma in a suit,
but what are you achieving by pretending
it doesn't touch you?)

When Mothra hatches from her Diet cocoon,
ethereal rupture, glitter fog,
amniotic gunge become new flesh,
the resurrection of the physical body is a spectacle,
a triumph.
Even the soldiers are awestruck

by the holy monstrosity,
the colossal moth rising, shrieking, from the ruins of its pupa.

The soup isn't formless
undifferentiated slop.
Rudiments persist as 'imaginal discs', clusters of
old flesh –
head, thorax, limbs and genitalia –
surviving the storm of potential.
Developmental biologists call it 'cell fate':
having lain dormant, the new body reaches
out from the grub's physical subconscious
and becomes what it would be if it
were existent.

Mothra doesn't think: Mothra *is*.
Its justice is automatic, a reflex or instinct.
When its priestesses are in danger, it knows what to do:
Protect furiously.
But unlike Godzilla, which is indestructible –
its every resurrection a cataclysm
(at least in the Heisei versus films of 1984-1995, which characterize
        Godzilla as a
terrifying, unpredictable enemy) –
Mothra's indestructibility and the inevitability of its rampages
are the indestructibility of hope,
the inevitability of goodness.

We know that moths remember being caterpillars. Well, maybe not
        exactly, but
there was a study where they showed that mature Lepidoptera

were averse to the smell of a chemical
(ethyl acetate, an industrial solvent often found in nail polish remover
and used for decaffeination)
because prior to metamorphosis any exposure to this smell
had been accompanied by an electric shock.
So torture shows that memory survives
insect transubstantiation.

(Saying that the moth body remembers its grub body
like steam remembers ice, like scar remembers wound
may be inaccurate, strictly speaking, but then,
I'm no entomologist.)

The body is a cloak –
shifting, malleable, opaque –
a mystery whose presence
obscures.
The word 'body' is the cloak
that, draped, hugging contours,
gives the mystery shape.

Does Mothra's larva know the pattern
that will decorate her wings?
Is her beauty in there from the beginning
buried, encoded, an imaginal disc
that, like the memory of torture, cannot disappear?

C O Z Z I L L A

burning reel a time by time re-stitched is boiling
        colours inhalation how the purple soaking
wreckage seems to be one way
        the world will end and as power lines
are falling we watch a drugged horizon bemused
        that so much is lost for so little
and can be dreamt anew as fantasy that blooms and yes
        the man on fire is a man on fire

        and the footage

taken from the shock of happening before distance
        renders it a *happened-then* of history and now

-watched with you in humid fogs of umber

and narcotic blue the blunder of a cheap magic
        trick is born again in terrible poetry

and it wades- a visible burning real

the white of clouds
behind the silver of planes

*

as looking down on looking up the aerial
         drone of opening on a city where the smoke is
ragged slow a portent drifting tired streets
         the crowded streets the grey and turning going on
that is the churning blood of streets
         and the boat below the bridge
with two children watching with their tiny hands
         on railings watching with

in what the desert breathes in cinders grid collapse

the blown orange never-seen, the gale of underworlds
         dropped from otherworlds in everywhere

of colour far beyond a colour to finish looking in the snow

*

         ash of after
         bodies

stripped and mineral forms of
and happened stillness mute

a cheap magic
trick is born again in
poetry, terrible

below the girders of a city torched

the unheard howl is coral

bleached through long-gone windows

trinite cinema

swelling in the rain of light

and remember fingers crumbling

a city

and over which

the lizard –

A CHILDHOOD FOR KAIJUS

and you are soft and good and full of wonder tonight. Like any other night of going unseen. Time is still opening for you, pouring across every branch, reaching to touch and thank whatever god made you in their image, creating a time where all the before the breakings can still be your now.

How many want to kill
Can you hold my palms without transgression

All parts of me are wrong
'Have you ever considered yourself expendable?'

The mountains yearn and birds sail over and smile at you. No one has ever called you innocent or even knew the word. Your earth still becoming under your feet.

Unblessed body
porous, hard skin
needy, fragile nails

All monsters are children again.

WATCHING PACIFIC RIM (2013) IN GENDER THERAPY

I am trying to become Woman again but I really want the monsters
        to win,
have a beach party, take a nap as the military sinks.

So much of me is empire; inside the film is the closest thing to flying
20 mins, I learn that my scales are bewildered; patents for a different
        present

I put my gender in the portal between human civilization and The
Breach. I am 22 when the Kaiju reach the land between my
        Childhood and my Queerness.

All the amour will close the gap
Forbid the possibility of other than this

When I bring my Kaiju into therapy
I remember Susan Stryker's words to Victor Frankenstein

Are we all just metal and water and metal in water
Oxidizing until our iron can be forged into something flesh

I put my ear to the sand, to the screen
Lust for growls, for tender, for me

ALEXANDRIA

When the city is coated in shadow; the kind that stains cement
between bricks,
the kind that waters eyes, and that breaks the news and air waves
and iPhones and
puts soles on the concrete. The librarian
follows their eight point plan, as do their staff, lanyards securely
around their necks,
and they paper cut themselves on books.

Spines are kissed and bound in brown paper and string. Muscle
memory overpowers
the need to scream, the need to weep, to shout, to pull out their
phones and call home,
but *this* is your home and how can this be happening *here* things
like this don't happen *here*
and they swallow sobs and barely breathe. The silence in the library
is magnified by the chaos; an echo of Alexandria.

Parcels are stacked before being tenderly gifted to the runners, the
staff who trained
weekly at park run and Wednesday night sports club. They blister
themselves
bloody. They swallow iron and snake themselves through the
streets, the city, through
the very veins of this country onto motorways and train tracks and
airports.
They hand out books like they're loaves of bread then

they run on and on and on and are only remembered by the colour
of their eyes or

the smell of their smile, or the sweaty finger prints that baptise the
paper to be later used

as book marks. The few survivors – because there are always so few
– read,

oh how they read. They tattoo their tongues with ink and times new
roman

sticks to their lenses inside their skulls. They read like our lives
depend on it.

MOTHRA SPOTTED IN THE NORTH OF ENGLAND,
MORE NEWS AT ELEVEN

At first they were placed under house arrest; curtains were stitched
shut. Half hourly
broadcasts protected the caricatures that the South had romanticised
and
soon enough everyone forgot that there are no fish in Whitby,
that's what the fishermen say. Or that there's no money in milk
farming
and it's the vegans' fault anyway, that's the rumour that runs rampant
through Lancashire.
Or that there are cars that get swept away by flash floods. Bodies too.
The half hourly broadcasts stretched to hourly, stretched to every
two hours,
stretched to once over breakfast then once over dinner. Soon enough
someone's curiosity stretched farther than expected
and they left their house.
And Mothra stayed in the sky, her wings outstretched in welcome.
She swooped and sailed
and, soon enough, more emerged from their homes. They drank in
the air that seemed cleaner,
ran across meadows teaming with life, and they followed
Mothra's shadow as she pirouetted over the Scarborough coast line
until the ocean was more fish than salt; they didn't question it, why
would they?
They bore witness to her rehoming dairy cows, who welcomed her
fluffy embrace,
and soon enough, people and homes and animals were protected
from flash floods;
nothing got swept away on narrow roads. Soon enough, the North of

England

forgot neglect from men in three piece suits and relatable checked

shirts.

Soon enough, they couldn't hear poor imitations of accents and

jokes about it being

bleak oop north

because it wasn't. It was beautiful.

ONE DAY MY EARS WILL STOP WORKING

One day my ears will stop working, I am sure of it. The drum
sticks
I've been white knuckling through life will shatter like bone
and I will be cotton wooled to the world. Maybe it won't be quite
like that,
maybe the live music events will take their toll, maybe
there's an hour glass in my head and I won't realise it's gone until
I'm choking on sand.

One day my ears will stop working, so I will learn sign language.
French was screamed at me
in school and my ear drums flinched with every misunderstood
syllable.
I make jokes that I *barely speaking English* because there's too
much snow and crackle
and static between a pause for breath. I want to King Kong people
and search through the voice box. I don't want destruction,
I just want to understand.

One day my ears will stop working but my hands won't; like his,
I'll pull apart
buildings and turns-of-phrase. I'll padlock my tongue, my voice
box;
my ear drums an audience to static, the same he hears,
but we'll be understood with sign language. I'm sure of it.

I'll know every inch of my lumbrical muscles, my flexor carpi ulnaris,

and I won't be confused by people again.

MORTE MEA, SPECIOSA

The old gods,
the gods of the sea,
are gone.

In their stead, the gods of money,
the gods of money,
the gods of money

***

all that we have
is the unforgotten
and the ocean
bombs the size of the sun
the city still
in the same spot
that a monster rose

***

To stop the bomb
we need to understand the monster
under their wings
like fish
like clouds
like rivers of people
in small things
the monster created by this small thing

requires the people
of the small place beneath them
to understand

***

and then again in greater
by these gods
to our destruction
as of course is always
meant to be but is
not necessary always
no but the ocean
will swallow
our greed
and our ambition
and our faith in monsters

***

In time
the gods will rise again
the old gods
the gods of the sea

but they will not
be gods
again
but will only be
what we ourselves
have become

***

In time
we will only know how
much we have destroyed
in the space of
our own small time
and our smaller gods
with this we should begin
by giving up our own
beliefs in the size of ourselves

***

In time
the monster will rise
to devour us
at last
but it will not be necessary
for we will be eaten away
bit by bit
as we consume ourselves

***

In time
we will be returned to
our own greatness
the gods of the sea
and they will rule
only as

we

rule

***

if you knew this

you would not have.

GOJIRA

Ancient, ashen sea.
Blossoms burn my eyes, crying,
'Rise, Gojira — rise.'

GLOBSTER

Something has washed up on the shore.
A mass of greying flesh, a lumpy silhouette,

with one string of carcass that could be a tentacle,
or embedded kelp, or a plesiosaur neck.

With the gravity of the uncategorisable,
saltwater is drawn around its chthonic body,

retreats, then returns for cyclical scrutiny.
Barnacle stars scattered across a sky of black skin

lead to a translucent flap, like the bulb of a jellyfish.
It could be an eye, or some other bloated organ,

slumping above a clump of jagged shells,
maybe teeth, maybe swallowed bones.

A curved tool, like a beak or a claw,
jabs two briny points into oozing sand.

The stink of death keeps the gulls wary.
There is a net, orange, obscene, wrapped

around its slender end. Blubber bursts
through tight diamonds of woven chains

stretching back into the sea, like Genesis.
One flabby island bears scars, perhaps a predator,

perhaps a propeller, and another is frothy
with plastic loops, squeezed by canless ripples.

Its dark, sleek hide shines like a mirror.
We should recognise monstrosity.

ECHIDNA

Daughter of disputed parentage, I was born
into deepest darkness. Anglerfish, eerie
midwives, held their candles as I burst
from the hide of a mermaid's purse, clawed
my way into this world, salt scorching
my navel as jaws ripped the chord.

My body is a contradiction, pale skin
slithering into scales, all of me shimmering,
aurora, terrifying. The poets scrambled
to write the unnatural horror of my beauty.
Harpy, hybrid, I had resigned myself
to a solitary life when Typhon found me.

The whirlpool of our coupling
pulled taut the corners of the world.
Afterwards, we floated, breathless,
blistered, my belly already curving
like an urn, ready to bear the image
of our monstrous children.

He stayed with me through all
my labours, when my tail would
thrash an avalanche, my body
ready to break for them, until
each screeching, sweating babe
was cradled in my coils.

My forked tongue licked at Orthus'
blood-slicked fur, each slobbering head
at a breast. Cerberus was trickier:
there was yapping and yowling
and nibbled ears for a turn at the nipple.
For Hydra we thought it best to give the bottle.

I suppose part of me knew
I was raising them for slaughter.
The gods ripped them from me,
sent them into service as soldiers,
as sentinels, as the plaything of heroes,
antagonists for theatre and odes.

Matriarch of a monstrous dynasty, I outlived
them all, made a cave out of my grief
and wept for them, alone again, ageless, aching.
I will linger here, until the ending of the world.
Mortals have always found a way to denounce
the different, and to kill the things they fear.

THE THING I AM

The Thing I Am awoke with a start. All was darkness. I was held tight, unable to move at first. As I struggled to free myself, I recalled my first awakening, though the place I had torn my way out of then had been warm and soft, instead of cold and stony. Suddenly, I yearned for it.

Pressing down upon me was a single great slab of rock, smoother and harder than any I remembered, my claws unable to penetrate its surface, or find its edges. Undeterred, I curled myself tight, and then with a thrust of my legs, I pushed up, moving the great slab just enough to expose its edges. Light poured in through the resulting gap, harsh and brilliant. The Thing I Am did not hesitate to thrust my talons into it, and drag myself up into that light.

What I found on the surface surprised the Thing I Am. The cave I had crawled into was at the top of a jagged mountain, protruding from the sea like one of my talons. What I had emerged from was a dark crater on a pancake flat island. Its sands felt hotter than they should have been, the dark stone crater hotter still. I wondered then how many eons I might have slept, and what had caused me to wake at last.

As waves crashed onto the island, the scent of the sea, heavy with salt and death, triggered a hunger in the Thing I Am, deep and sorrowful as the oceans themselves. I recalled the creatures the Thing I Am, and things like me, used to feast upon. The largest of them dwelled beneath the waves, many times larger even than us. Though they were soft and weak compared to things like me, their sheer scale, and the speed and grace with which they could navigate the ocean depths, meant it would take four or five of us to slay one before it could escape. We would drag its carcass up onto the land and feast together upon it, bathing in its crimson juices. There would be so much of it we would not have to fight for our share.

The Thing I Am recalled the feeling of being with other things like me. In darkness and in silence, I could still feel they were there. When we feasted together on sea creatures it was a warm feeling, like that first place the Thing I Am had emerged from.

I could feel no other things like me now. The world was calm and desolate. The island I had emerged from was desolate too, devoid even of creatures to hunt. For a moment the Thing I Am wondered if the whole world might be like this now; if the Thing I Am had awoken too soon, before the world had recovered from the burning skies which had instigated its decline. The Thing I Am considered crawling back into the crater, sealing the lustrous black rock, and returning to my slumber, but at that thought my body ached with hunger.

Then another thought came to the Thing I Am. There must be other things like me, still sleeping somewhere inside the earth. If I could become strong enough, perhaps they would feel me, just as I had once felt them, and wake. Then we would hunt together again, and the world would feel warm and red. The Thing I Am needed to feed.

I unfurled my wings. They ached after eons without use. I ignored the pain, and flapped them hard, but failed to take off from the ground. The Thing I Am let out a scream, but my voice, too, was atrophied and hollow. I tried again and again, rage building in me, and at last that rage lifted me up, the buzzing of it in my brain filling the void left by the absence of other things like me, but only for a moment.

As I rose above the clouds I felt an initial sense of disappointment. Before my sleep, and before their burning, the skies had teemed with winged creatures, constantly swooping and diving as they hunted and fought with one another. While they were small compared to things like me, they were large enough to provide some sustenance, and easy to catch besides. While the skies I soared in now were not entirely empty, the creatures I found there were tiny, soft things. They seemed almost petulant, as they flitted close to me in strange triangular formations. I lashed out at them, but they were so small they slipped between my talons, cackling as they went.

I flew higher, to where I could hear their mocking no more. The higher I went, the more endless the seas seemed. More and more bitter blue rolled out before me. If the world had been so empty when the Thing I Am had gone to sleep, I did not remember it as such. At last, sudden as it was slow, something appeared on the horizon; the unmistakable green of land. In an instant I pivoted in the air, and dived headlong towards it.

The Thing I Am did not try to slow my descent, instead relishing the thunder of my feet crashing down. I imagined my prey scattering in all directions, duly terrified, unlike the tiny white winged pests which had mocked me.

Before the skies had burned, all the land was green, and filled with the creatures things like me fed upon, and the creatures they had fed upon in turn. The Thing I Am had delighted in wading knee deep through the trees, hunting the largest of them; those vicious or proud enough to try to fight back. I would allow them to bite and claw at me for a while, until their teeth, and their spirits, were broken. Then they would at last turn to run, and I would strike.

I would drag the creature into a clearing and wait, knowing that the other things like me would have felt the kill, and would come. If too many came I would have to fight for a share of my own kill, but I didn't mind; it made the feeling of being together all the more intense. It was rare for the other things like me to do the same. When they made a kill they seemed to feast as quickly as they could, and would often be gone before the Thing I Am arrived, but I didn't mind that either.

Then the skies had burned, and with them much of the green. After the fire came ice, a cold which could not harm things like me, but further diminished the green. As the land turned cold, all white and grey, the creatures we hunted became more scarce, as did the creatures they hunted in turn. It was then that our hunger had increasingly forced us from the land to the seas, where we had to hunt in packs of four or five to bring down even one of the giant creatures which lived there. As we had feasted upon them, drenched in crimson juices, more things like me would crash down from the skies, and unlike before, they would have to fight for a share. This too, I did not mind.

After a time though, the sea creatures dwindled in number too. The Thing I Am felt terrible hunger almost all of the time, and when a kill was made, more things like me descended upon it than could possibly win a sufficient share. The fighting became more and more vicious, and sometimes things like me would kill each other. More than once the Thing I Am killed another thing like me, but its meat tasted too bitter and sad to eat, despite the terrible hunger I felt. Worse still, while I could still feel the other things like me, that feeling was no longer exciting, or warm; it was as cold and discomforting as the barren earth. Slowly even that feeling faded, and I encountered fewer and fewer things like me, so I had found my dark stony womb, and gone to sleep.

Now I stood again on green land, but it wasn't the same as before the skies burned. The trees were small and sparse, and the creatures which darted between them were smaller still, less like those the Thing I Am once feasted upon, than those they hunted in turn. They were too tiny to sustain a thing like me.

For a second time since my awakening, the Thing I Am turned my head to the sky and screamed, but still it sounded hollow.

The Thing I Am took to the skies once more, and in the distance, further inland, I saw a great grey expanse. There, I thought, I would find a new cave to crawl into, and despite my hunger I would rest. Perhaps I would sleep again, to wait until the world was ready for a thing like me again, or to wake nevermore.

I glided languidly towards the grey wastes, when suddenly a huge, white creature, with streaks of red on its tail, dived past me. It was larger even than the sky creatures the Thing I Am had hunted before the skies had burned.

It was fast, and in a moment of stunned disbelief I had allowed it to escape me, but that was of no concern. Instead of giving chase

I dipped beneath the clouds and watched, as it landed in the same grey lands I had been heading towards.

When I caught up with the big white winged creature it was laying unmoving on the ground, refusing even to lash out at smaller flightless creatures which now swarmed around it. I wondered if it might be a thing more like me than the creatures I used to hunt; with skin too thick to worry about such minor nuisances. I decided that I needed to test it.

The Thing I Am flew high above the clouds again, so as to remain hidden from the creature, and positioned myself directly above it. In this way I knew that if it fled, it would have no head start, no matter what direction it tried to escape in. Only then did I begin my descent.

I partially retracted my wings, so as I dropped they would fill with air and slow my descent. Closer and closer to the ground I drifted, and yet the creature still did not react. I wondered if I was still too far off for it to see, until other, smaller creatures began to let out shrill screams, some scattering into the distance, others fixed in place. Still the creature didn't move. Perhaps it really was a thing like me, or at least something similar, something new which had emerged during my eons of slumber; self assured and welcoming of the fight ahead. If so, the Thing I Am would not disappoint it.

I pulled my wings in close to me now, and allowed myself to hurtle towards the creature, faster and faster, propelled by hunger and rage. I crashed down upon it, breaking its back and biting down onto its neck, but no satisfying crimson juices met my lips.

The creature was cold and tasteless, its hard exterior was not flesh like that of the creatures I used to hunt, but a carapace made of something not quite shell, not quite stone, but just as unsatisfying as either for the Thing I Am to bite upon. I screamed and began to tear at it with my claws, hoping to find something better inside.

What I did find surprised the Thing I Am. Inside the great white creature with the wings, were dozens of the small, flightless ones which had crowded around it. I wondered if they might be some kind of parasite which had infected it, but even as I did, hunger overtook the Thing I Am. Before I could consider the ramifications, I found myself tearing the white creature in half, turning its newly exposed insides upwards so nothing could spill out, and beginning to feast upon the smaller creatures within. They made satisfying screams as I plucked them out by the handful, each too tiny to offer much nourishment, but collectively a pleasure to grind together with my hind teeth.

When the white carapace was empty, the Thing I Am threw it down, and this time gave a roar of delight, rather than a frustrated scream. I looked around me. More of the little creatures rushed in all directions, and I pounced on one of them. Its tiny body was crushed by the power of my claws, and the crimson sludge which remained was barely worth the effort it took to lift it to my lips. The Thing I Am realized that to sustain myself, and become strong enough to awaken the other things like me, I needed to find these tiny creatures where they clustered together, like in the white carapace.

The Thing I Am unfurled my wings once more, and this time lifted easily off of the ground, but not far. I rose up just high enough to see over the strange angular hillocks the tiny creatures seemed to have burrowed into, and there I discovered not one, but dozens of the large white winged creatures, each with different markings on its tail, but unmistakably of the same kind.

The Thing I Am wondered how I had ever thought these docile white things could have been something akin to a thing like me, as I pounced upon the closest of them. This time I knew where to pierce the carapace with my claws, and it came apart with ease. I turned the open end upward just as I had before, careful not to spill any of the tiny creatures out, but I found it empty.

In my rage, the Thing I Am flung it at another of the dormant white winged creatures, and to my surprise both burst into flame, like a miniature recreation of the day the sky burned. The display did not placate me. I delighted in the thunderous sound of my feet on the ground, which cracked beneath me as I ran towards the next white winged creature. I told myself I would tear open every one of them until I had my fill of the little parasites which dwelled inside, but before I reached it, there was another sound, and then a stinging on my back.

I turned to see a group of the tiny creatures which, rather than running from me, were slowly coming towards me. They were accompanied by some new kind of creature, encased in a similar carapace to the winged ones, but smaller, green and flightless. It had something like a long beak or trunk protruding from it. As I examined it, the trunk flashed with flame, and I felt its sting again, this time on my chest.

I recalled the most proud and vicious of the land creatures I had hunted before the burning of the skies, how they would try to fight me with their impotent little claws and teeth, and I felt a wave of excitement.

I flew at the squat green creature, and slashed at its trunk. The Thing I Am was surprised that while my blow knocked it to one side, it did not immediately break. It didn't matter. I would tear it apart one piece at a time if I had to. I would delight in doing so, and then I would taste the tiny parasites inside. Perhaps then the other things like me would feel me, and wake. I was impatient now for them to do so.

As I grabbed the squat green creature's trunk, and began to twist it off, it flashed again, but this time rather than stinging me, its fires struck one of the angular rocks the tiny creatures had burrowed into. As flames engulfed a burrow, tiny creatures burst out from it. Rather than pounce on them immediately, I decided to watch, as an understanding grew in me of how best to hunt this new prey. In their delicious panic the tiny creatures clambered over one another, even pushed each other to the ground, and the Thing I Am realized they would barely require any hunting at all. In their terror they would pile themselves up for me to pluck from the ground, just as they did now. All except one.

The tiny creatures were a homogenous mass, indistinguishable from one another, apart from that one. It was clearly of their kind, the same size and shape as the others, but it was wrapped in what appeared to be a kind of flightless wing of brilliant scarlet, and on its head was a plumage the golden color of the midday sun. This one seemed to stop, to pull others of its kind up from under the pile, though it knew I was there. The Thing I Am stopped to watch it for a moment, and it in turn watched me, all while it worked to free an especially tiny parasite from the pile, and then wrap it in its flightless wings.

The Thing I Am recalled once more the warm place I had first emerged from, and the feeling of other things like me, when we feasted on some great carcass together, but my reminiscing was cut short as I felt another sting, and another, and then yet more.

I turned to see three more of the squat green creatures coming towards me, surrounded by parasites, which seemed to have grown little trunks of their own, protruding from their limbs. All of them flashed and stung in turn. The Thing I Am wanted to rush towards them, to let them see how futile their stinging trunks were, just as I had allowed the creatures I had once hunted to break their teeth upon my hide, so they could know fear before I consumed them. But I did not. For some reason I did not quite understand, the Thing I Am instead unfurled my wings, and took to the sky once more.

In the distance I made out the shape of a great mountain, the kind which had existed since before the skies were burned, and I headed towards it. There I made my perch, and the Thing I Am unleashed my rage upon its rocky face, hacking with claws, biting with teeth and swinging with my tail, but even things like me cannot break the earth itself. When my rage was spent, I considered what I had learned. I had learned that the tiny parasites amassed not only inside the larger, armored creatures, but also, and perhaps in greater number, within the burrows they made in the strange, angular rocks. I had learned that fear would drive them into those burrows, but flame would drive them out again. I had learned that some of them would push their kind down in their desperation to escape me, while others, rarer ones like the creature of scarlet and gold, would stop to help them up again. In either case they made themselves easy pickings for me. Finally, I had learned that the strange trunks which sometimes protruded from them could sting, but not harm, a thing like me.

The Thing I Am recalled the sensation of pouring the little parasites into my jaws, and grinding out their juices with my hind teeth. The Thing I Am imagined how much sweeter still the red and gold creature would have tasted. Its plumage had been the color of midday sun, but now the sun was sinking, and under the paler light of the moon, the Thing I Am would find out. Tonight, I would use all the things I had learned, and the Thing I Am would feast, and make the other things like me awaken again.

I flew high above the grey mass of land where the tiny parasites made their burrows, and searched for the largest of the strange, angular rock formations. I found them at the center of the grey lands. They were taller than they were wide, like giant tree trunks or small, flat topped mountains, far larger even than the Thing I Am. There was a shine to them, and the light of the moon reflected off of them, reminiscent of how sunlight had played upon the shiny black stone beneath which I had awakened. I hung on my wings, just above the tallest of them. Beneath me I heard frightened noises. Some of the tiny parasites had noticed my presence, but not enough of them, not yet.

I allowed my eyes to drink in moonlight for a moment, and my lungs to drink in the cold night air, and then from inside of me the Thing I Am unleashed something the like of which the world had surely not seen during the long eons of my sleep, not since things like me had fought each other for the last scraps of food on a dying world. The Thing I Am unleashed my fiery breath.

The flat top of the giant angular rock was immediately blasted open, made jagged and pointed like the true mountains of old. The shining surfaces which had covered the rock, and protected the burrows of the parasites, shattered all at once, falling like rain on the creatures which had gathered below and sending up a scent which reminded me of my hunger. Everything was ablaze. With a satisfied growl, I descended.

The parasites had already begun flooding out of their burrows in terror, just has they had before. As they emerged, panicked and blinded by smoke, I scooped them up by the handful, gleeful as I ground them up with my hind teeth.

The green, squat creatures with the trunks were quick to come this time, but I knew their stinging could not harm me, so I took turns between filling my mouth with the tiny parasites, and dismembering my shelled attackers between bites. Other creatures came too. Some whirred about my head, and others shrieked through the sky, faster perhaps even than I. They all had their own versions of the stinging trunks, and I swatted all of them aside, crashing them into the burrows they sought to defend, creating further blazes, and forcing more and more of the parasites out into the open, for the Thing I Am to feast upon.

And then at last, as I bathed in destruction, and feasted on crimson juices, I felt it. I felt another thing like me, somewhere in the dark. It felt warm and hungry. Somehow, I knew it was not quite awake yet, but awakening, stirring because it felt the Thing I Am too, in my glory and my rage. The feeling filled me with an unexpected fear.

In an instant I saw how small the world had become since I had last hunted upon it. If the other thing like me awoke, it would not be the last. At first we would feast together, and feel each other's presence, warm and intense, as of old. Others would feel our presence too, and then more still, until all the things like me which slept within the earth joined us, and the world would feel as it had in those times, before the skies had burned.

But the Thing I Am also knew that the world was more fragile than it had been then. The tiny creatures, the parasites, whether they dragged each other down, or lifted each other up, would render themselves equally vulnerable, and fall at our feet.

Soon their numbers would dwindle, and once more the things like me would fight amongst ourselves for what scraps remained. The world would taste bitter once more, and once more we would be forced to sleep, diminished further this time than the last.

And the tiny creatures? They would have been devoured for less than nothing.

As I rose up into the skies once more, the Thing I Am thought, for the briefest moment, that I caught a glimpse of that one with the flightless scarlet wings, and plumage as gold as the midday sun. If I had, then it would see me now too; a dark tarnish on the pale full moon.

Dawn had begun to break as I reached the pancake island where I had awakened, and back into its stony womb I crawled. With a blast of my breath I melted the strange black stone, and sealed myself within. Whatever had awakened me, it had done so too soon. Now, the Thing I Am would sleep again, for untold eons more. So would the other things like me, waiting for the world to be ready for things like us again. Until then, I would dream of scarlet and gold, and I would yearn once more.

MOTHRA READS THE COP28 AGREEMENT

The conference convenes in a petrostate. A great egg appears on an island.

OPEC is in attendance, its members shake delegates' hands, steer by the elbow. The egg hatches.

Mothra searches the text for *phase out*, finds only *transition to*. Spots CCUS inserted like the chimerical fricative in her name.

Mothra crosses the ocean.

Mothra sees rehashed promises to *accelerate efforts towards phase-down of coal*, spins a cocoon from offcuts of progress and discarded hope.

Mothra reads *inefficient subsidies*, hears ready-made excuses dripping from slick-mouthed men in suits. Discovers acceptance of *loss and damage* but no money for places like her blasted home, its shrinking green island within an island.

Mothra knows underestimation, had to birth a male to be called lion; yet it is the females of the pride who hunt, and she has decimated cities.

Mothra spies *transitional fuels* attempting to blend in, clutching an attaché case.

Mothra takes to the sky.

GODZILLA'S MAN-CRUSH

I heard a story about a girl
who used to stay awake at night
thinking she'd turn into a painting.
She said she wouldn't be able to talk
to people anymore.

I envisioned this as my perfect desert island,
made from my favourite dessert -
a place no one understands
but pretends to understand,
like how fibre comes from fruit
or talking about the milky way
without thinking of chocolate.

I agree -
I think aliens do exist
and watch us when we were dinosaurs
when dinosaurs discussed poetry -
not butter
and complain about the use of lemons in water,
and won't admit how crap
gin and tonic really tastes.

It's not like something from a film
it's like childbirth
for a child -
a person's abstract painting
in reverse
splattered all over Camden
like unswallowed puke.

OUTDOOR MORGUE

How to eat breakfast outside when you don't want to.
Flowers on my wallpaper. It's not a happy thing.
When I'm awake, people chatting at me, I see the evolution of mould,
devolution of flowers, flowers that bloom,
then wrinkle, then dust.

I smoke cigarettes so I can experience the dust in my lungs.
Get high from breathing wintered air, grow lilies in my organs,
let them grow mould together, fungi inside out, organs and mind,
mind monster.

Climb the walls with friendly chaos, telling the world
my own private bonkers on Mr. Facebook,
singing to no one,
screaming at everyone
with my mouth shut
smiling.
Scale the largest cathedral on hand,
shoot at people with swear words,
have everyone shoot me whilst carrying the love of my life
towards the night sky,
fall to my perfect death as she watches.

She'll watch
and cry
for my falling corpse.

That's what I hope happens.

STAY PUFT

My old best mate from school.

I guess I, and all of us, have all had more than one of those.

a kid whose parents had split up. He said his mum works at Tesco's

and never sees his dad.

This means he had the whole Ghostbusters toys collection,

and I just had Slimer.

He even had the giant marshmallow fucker we all wanted to eat.

I think we even watched Ghostbusters 2 together. I definitely

        dreamt of the

giant marshmallow man coming after us. I was hiding behind a

        ramp – fuck knows why.

I was hiding with my mum. My dad was someplace safe watching

        the telly.

My mate says his dad was gonna save him. I swear that's all I

        remember of his dad.

My mate with his tears and puke. My mum making him marmite

        sandwiches,

whilst he eyed up all my toys.

I think he became a bank manager, or something.

MANDA

The first death we suffered was constriction. Didn't I say,
as the weapons console burst and the headboard cracked,
that this was the doing of the people of Mu – who, by the way,
do not exist, and whose empire never sank, in point of fact
(since if it had, there would remain some smeary echo of it)
and who, to keep their lack of existence secret
from those who would think it something to covet,
magicked into being a guardian, part god, part sea krait,
with the flewed snout and teeth of a dog-dragon,
the barbels of the Mekong catfish, a lionfish's spined frills,
and for a body, the long, brass belt of a machinegun,
but unfathomably vast, such that the undulations of its gills
could crush a trawler – such that it could not stay hidden
even in the abyssal trenches of the Pacific,
but grew to enclose the whole world within its cordon,
and has now grown old, and worm-brained, and seasick.
Didn't I say this, as one length of one coil of that beast
tightened about us, and the clouds began to crumple,
and you and I and all the others were compressed
to a mere sliver of diamond, to an ampoule?

WHO THE F*** IS GORGO?

The first time I saw the Monster Man, I was nine years old.

Back then, it'd been just Mum and me. She was significantly older than all my friends' mums, but I wouldn't notice that until years later, when I became a teenager. At nine years old and with a sense of self that was still squishy and unformed, when I looked at my mother all I saw was my best friend and the kookiest, most interesting person on the planet. The world hadn't jaded me yet, and so I couldn't see her for what she really was; a flagging, ageing mother doing her best to fill my childhood with as many sparkling memories as possible.

Before she'd had me, Mum had had an impressive career in London. Doing what exactly, I didn't know, but I'd once seen an old photo of her sitting at a desk, typing onto a boxy computer and grinning over her shoulder at the camera person, all shoulder pads and lipstick. But then she got pregnant with me, so she ditched the career, moved to a quiet town in Essex and opened a small pottery studio. When I'd asked her why she gave up her old life, she'd said, 'London is a fabulous, intoxicating place, darling. But it's full of weirdos. It's no place to raise a family. You need to grow up here, among normal people.'

That's how she always referred to the two of us: a family. Privately, I often wondered if her desire for a family could ever really be fulfilled by just one geeky kid.

Despite loving her new, quiet life in Essex ('my second act!'), Mum could never stay away from London for long. Several times a year, the two of us would bundle onto the train to Liverpool Street and we'd spend the day acting like tourists – visiting the free museums or wandering around Camden market and haggling with the stall holders. One time, we snuck into the London Palladium and caught the second half of *The King and I*.

Personally, I wasn't crazy about London. It was loud and dirty. But Mum loved the city, and I loved her.

On the evening that I first saw the Monster Man, Mum and I had been to the Tate Modern. We were sitting on a bench overlooking the Thames, sharing a bag of chips and a can of Dr Pepper as the sun slowly set over the water. To our left was the Millenium Bridge, which was still cordoned off from the public. It had been unveiled a couple of months earlier, only to be quickly re-veiled when everybody realised that walking across it caused it to wobble and creak to a concerning degree, like the whole thing was about to collapse into the river.

'I just don't *get it,* though! Like how is it art if you just paint a canvas blue? Or stick a football in a plastic tank? I could do that!'

'Art is supposed to be divisive, darling. The fact that we're still talking about those pieces means that the artists did their job.'

'Their job is stupid!'

'Be respectful, darling,' Mum said, but she was laughing too. She promptly stopped when she saw him.

He was homeless, I think. The signs were all there – ragged clothes worn in layers, messy hair in need of a wash, and ruddy, weather-worn skin. As he ambled past us, I noticed that his gait was unbalanced, like he was having trouble orienting himself in this plane of existence. I felt the fifty pence piece in my cardigan pocket, the change left over from our dinner.

'Shall we give him some money, Mum?' I whispered. She didn't look away from the man, just shook her head stiffly and patted my shoulder, which I took as an instruction to sit quietly until the man shuffled away to somewhere else.

But he didn't. He dumped his ratty backpack on the pavement in front of us, pulled out a large aerosol can and approached the tourist information sign that was a couple of meters to our left. I gasped. This adult man was about to graffiti in broad daylight, right in front of us!

Sure enough, he began to spray a thin, concentrated line of bright green paint onto the sign, rendering the tourist map completely useless.

I was expecting Mum to do something. She never usually missed an opportunity to stand up for what was right and always encouraged me to do the same, but on that evening, she didn't say a word to the man, just watched him keenly and kept her hand on my shoulder, anchoring me.

After a minute or so, there was shouting behind us and two large men ran into view, knocking the spray can out of the Monster Man's hand and roughly tackling him to the ground. They were wearing matching uniforms and so I assumed they were brutalizing him in a professional capacity, but that didn't make it any less terrifying for nine-year-old me. I scooched closer to Mum. The bag of chips fell off my lap and scattered across the pavement.

With the three men tussling on the ground, I had a clear view of the fresh graffiti. The artwork was messy, but it appeared to be a strange sort of lizard monster with distinctive webbed ears, standing tall on its hind legs with a thick tail raised out behind. It kind of looked like a poor man's Godzilla.

Suddenly, the Monster Man broke free and sprinted towards the Millenium Bridge. With surprising agility for a man in his late forties, he hoisted himself over the metal railing and began running across the bridge, which creaked loudly under him. One of the uniformed men yelled something into a walkie-talkie. The other simply watched in tired disbelief.

'Remember Gorgo!' the Monster Man screamed.

Who's Gorgo? I wondered.

***

The second time that I saw the Monster Man, I was 15 years old and having a panic attack.

It was my friend Anna's fault. Our favourite band, Trashed Sanity, had announced a gig at the Brixton Academy and she decided that we needed to be there. Neither of us had ever been to a proper gig before, much less one in London, but she'd convinced me that if we missed it, we would spend the rest of our lives drowning in regret.

'These guys are American; they never play UK gigs! If we don't go this, who knows how long it'll be until they come back here? If ever?!'

'I guess,' I mumbled. 'But there's no way our parents will let us go. Brixton's well rough.'

So I'd heard, anyway. As a fairly sheltered teenager, most of my opinions were borrowed from other people.

'I'll say to my parents that I'm sleeping over at yours. You can tell your mum you're staying at mine if you want, but let's be honest – she's not gonna notice if you're home or not.'

Ouch. She was right, though. At that point in time, Mum and I were existing in a sort of purgatory era in her illness where she spent most of her time dosed up on strong medication, but nobody had realised yet that she'd become too sick to look after me. She would lose track of things all the time, namely my whereabouts.

'Okay. Yeah, let's do it,' I said, forcing a smile. Anna squealed.

The night had been incredible, at first. We caught the train to Liverpool Street without issue, successfully navigated the tube and walked from Brixton station to the venue which was, to our delight, teeming with eccentric adults sporting mohawks, piercings and leather jackets, filling the air with songs and swear words. It all felt very illicit and cool.

About halfway into Trashed Sanity's set, I began to panic. Anna and I had pushed our way right to the front of the crowd and the only thing separating us from the stage was a thick metal barrier. At first, I'd been having a brilliant time – the music was pulsing through my entire body and was loud enough to drown out both my off-key singing and my anxiety about lying to Mum. But then I made the mistake of glancing over my shoulder at the vast sea of moshers behind me. They all looked so rowdy, aggressively headbanging and shoving one another, losing themselves in the music in the most violent way possible. I was suddenly aware of the hundreds of bodies pressed against mine, compressing my lungs, ramming me harder and harder into the metal barrier, not caring that they were strong, drunk adults and I was a small teenage girl in danger of breaking.

And then there were hands in my armpits, and I was being lifted into the air by a security guy, plucked from the pulsing hivemind like a chosen one. As my body was peeled away from hundreds of others, I could hear somebody asking if I was okay and another person asking for a bottle of water. I knew that Anna was still caught in the maelstrom, but in that moment, I didn't care if I never saw her again. All I knew was that I had to get the hell out of there.

Outside, night had settled in, but Brixton didn't care. Cars were roaring down the road, pedestrians were shouting across the street at each other in a way that could be either hostile or playful, and the muffled beat of Trashed Sanity's music was thumping through the air. As I stumbled down the steps of the venue and braced myself on one of the stone pillars to catch my breath, it became painfully clear to me that I wasn't illicit and cool at all, I was just some stupid Essex kid in a city full of terrifying adults.

Without Mum by my side, I had no buffer against London's filth and chaos. More than anything, I wished I could be back in our cosy little flat, sitting at her bedside and reading to her from *That's Life!* magazine while she rested her eyes, instead of having a breakdown in the street and trying not to vomit.

And that's when I saw him. He was just over the road, examining a brick wall next to a betting shop. There was a tin of lime green emulsion paint at his feet, the sort that you'd use to paint your sitting room walls, only he was using it to decorate the wall with a messy painting of a massive reptilian monster, the same one that he'd painted over the sign next to the Millenium Bridge six years earlier.

Perhaps it was because I wasn't thinking straight, or because he was the one familiar thing amidst the chaos, but as soon as I saw him, I went to him.

'What are you painting?'

He flinched at the sound of my voice; the monster now had a

jagged tail. When he turned to look at me, our eyes didn't quite meet – it was like he couldn't focus his gaze on anything for more than a second, like something in his mind was off-balance and scrambling for purchase, as out of place in the city as I was.

When he spoke, he had an Irish accent.

'This is Gorgo. Nobody remembers him.'

'They don't?'

'No. They don't.' He dunked the paintbrush into to green-stained tin and brushed a fresh line of paint over the monster's tail, smoothing out the jagged part.

'Who's Gorgo?'

The Monster Man turned to me. His eyes flitted upwards and a small hint of a smile passed over his face, like the opportunity had finally arrived for him to tell a story that he'd been holding in for far too long.

'Well, I'll tell you. When I was a boy, my parents both passed, Lord have mercy on their souls. We were from Galway, in west Ireland, but when they passed I ended up on a little island called Nara, just off the coast. I was working for a Mr McCartin, the harbour master. Just little jobs here and there that a wee child could do.

'Anyways, I'd been on the island a couple of months when I woke in my bed one night because of a big noise out in the water. I went outside and there was a sea spirit in the bay, a big, hulking thing with thick scales and red eyes, and she told me her name was Ogra. She was big like, but not a bit scary, not for me. We got to be friends, her and me.

'So, months go by, and one day these two English fellas come sailing up to the island, shipwrecked, they said. They were wanting some repairs on their boat, but they were a little rude to the fellas at the harbour and nobody really thought much of them. I was eager to see the back of them, myself.

'Well wouldn't you know, their first night on the island, a sea spirit comes out of the water to say hello. At first I'd thought it was Ogra but no, it was too small, only just as tall as the rooftops. It was Ogra's wee babby. He wasn't harming anyone, just stamping about and roaring a bit, having a little fun there, but all the fellas got scared and started attacking him, and that got *him* scared. And then, these two wicked English fellas captured the poor thing and shipped him off to London! Can you believe? Doing a thing like that to an innocent babby?'

The Monster Man was getting worked up. He was gesturing wildly with the paintbrush, splashing lime green paint onto the pavement and my boots, earning puzzled glances from passers-by. I took a step back from him. He promptly filled the gap.

'And d'you know what they did when they got the babby here, to London? They threw him in a cage and put him on display like a damn circus animal! Named him Gorgo, meaning 'monster', they said. Cruel, wicked people. I saw the whole thing, you know. I'd stowed away on their boat, 'cause I knew I had to keep an eye on Ogra's wee babby for her.'

I kept inching backwards, but he wasn't taking the hint. Any further, and I'd be in the road.

'And it was a good thing I was there! I called Ogra the way I used to on Nara Island, and she came swimming up the Thames to collect her little Gorgo. These people, these English,' he gestured widely at the surrounding pedestrians and almost hit one in the face, who swore loudly but still carried on their way. 'They brought in the army boys, and they tried to kill them both! But Ogra's tough, and she got back in the Thames, and she took her babby home. The whole city was in uproar, it was all over the news at the time.'

I stumbled off the curb.

'But d'you know the worst of it? This whole fecking city has amnesia! 1961, that all happened, and I've been here ever since. Nobody remembers! 'Who's Gorgo?' they say. They say I want throwing in the looney bin! They're the looney ones, forgetting a thing like that!'

My memory of the next part is jumbled. I remember backing away from the Monster Man, who'd become so agitated that he was spitting as he shouted. I remember his watery blue eyes finally finding mine. I remember being hit by something and my body momentarily flying through the night air, then smacking against the road and pain exploding through my left shoulder.

There was a lot of yelling and footsteps. The street was tilting back and forth, strange voices were slipping in and out of focus and the coppery stink of blood was rising around me. I remember lying in the road, my cheek against the cold tarmac, watching the Monster Man amble up the street and eventually becoming lost in the sea of pedestrians, leaving behind a trail of lime green paint droplets on the pavement.

***

The final time that I saw the Monster Man, I was 29 years old and depressed.

Part of the reason for my depression was the fact that I'd ended up living in London. I know, I know. Moving to the city hadn't exactly been part of my life plan, but when Mum died, I realised there was no such thing as a life plan. You can't plot out your life like the chapters of a book. Shit happens, go with it.

Anyway, with Mum gone and my carer's allowance halted, there was nothing left for me in Essex, so I put a deposit down on the first grotty little flat I could find in East London, and I quickly moved in. New city, new start? Perhaps I just wanted to feel close to Mum again.

London is supposed to be one of the most exciting cities on our planet and maybe it is, if you're a tourist. But if you're a resident? No. The overpopulation is so out of control that after a few weeks of living here, other human beings become simply part of the backdrop; objects to shove past or step over, rather than sentient beings with whom you could maybe share a joke or fall in love. And if you do swallow your pride and attempt to speak to one of them, they look at you like you're crazy – why are you bothering them when you could be looking at your phone, like a normal person?

It's such a lonely, loud place.

From day one in the city, I'd been keeping an eye out for the Monster Man, but years passed without a single sighting.

The Gorgo paintings, however, were everywhere. The only trouble was that the city was absolutely covered in graffiti, and so unless you were actively looking for Gorgos, they would be easy to miss. But I knew to look for them. I'd see them on public walls, phone boxes, bus shelters, the pavement... one time in Camden, I'd even caught a glimpse of a tiny Gorgo scrawled in marker pen on the back of some punk rocker's denim jacket.

But the Monster Man was right; nobody else in the city noticed the Gorgo paintings or remembered the incident from 1961. If I ever mentioned the subject with my colleagues or neighbours, they would all give me the same look, that one that made me clam up and stop making people uncomfortable.

It wasn't just the Londoners who were determined to forget Gorgo. The internet was equally obtuse. It was bizarre; each time I typed the word 'Gorgo' into the search engine, it brought up zero results. Not a bunch of unrelated websites, literally a blank screen. I'd never seen that happen before.

It was enough to make me feel like I was losing my mind. Did the Monster Man even exist, or had I imagined him? And if he was real, why was I so invested in something he'd probably made up or hallucinated?

But deep down, I knew he'd been telling the truth. Gorgo was real, he had to be.

When I finally saw the Monster Man again, it was in very mundane circumstances. It was a sunny, midweek lunchtime and I was sitting on a bench in Battersea Park, eating a supermarket sandwich and trying to get interested in the crime novel that I was reading. My eyes strayed over the top of the book and that's when I spotted him, crouched in front of the large peace pagoda opposite me, doodling Gorgo in thick black marker onto its stone wall. I dropped the book and the sandwich and rushed over to him.

'It's you!' I exclaimed.

He glanced up at me with zero recognition, then continued defacing the pagoda.

'You don't remember me?' My stomach sank. 'Brixton? 14 years ago? I got hit by a car?'

Still nothing.

'Gorgo?' I tried.

That did it. He stood up and his face illuminated with joy, but his eyes were still not quite meeting mine.

'You remember Gorgo?' he gasped.

Hesitantly, I nodded. He just about burst with excitement. For a horrifying moment I thought he was about to hug me, but instead he ran past me, leapt over the wall of the pagoda with surprising agility for a man in his late sixties, and landed heavily on the path below, which bordered a rather peaceful section of the Thames. He was heading to the water.

'Come on!' he yelled over his shoulder.

By the time I reached edge of the river, he was already up to his waist in the water. I squinted. He was fiddling with something in his hand, perhaps a small instrument of some sort... an ocarina? A harmonica? My eyesight wasn't good enough.

He brought the instrument to his lips and blew into it. A deafening, monstrous noise erupted from the tiny thing, a horrific combination of a lion's roar and an elephant's bellow, sending a thick ripple across the water and ruffling the grass on both sides of the riverbank. Instinctively I covered my ears and steeled myself for what would inevitably happen next.

A circular ripple appeared in the middle of the river, gradually spreading and giving way to more ripples, until the surface broke and an enormous, ghostly beast rose up from the riverbed, bellowing out the same monstrous call that the Monster Man had mimicked, like it had been rudely awoken from a decades-long slumber. The creature was unmistakeable. Webbed ears, thick scales, and red, unblinking eyes. Its strong tail smacked against the surface of the water and sent a small tidal wave crashing against the riverbank that I was standing on, drenching me to my bones.

Gorgo.

The Monster Man cheered and danced in the water.

There were other people in park – a couple of joggers, a picnicking family, a few other lunchtime office workers – but none of them reacted at all to the towering river monster. It was as if they were all in a trance, and the Monster Man and I were the only ones who were awake.

I stared up at the beast and tried to formulate a coherent reaction, but my brain was short-circuiting and there was only one thing ringing out in my mind. Gorgo was real! We weren't crazy!

A memory came to me, something that Mum had said in her final days. By that time, the illness had ravaged her so thoroughly that her voice had been paper-thin, struggling under the weight of her own words, but it seemed very important to her that I heard this final thought.

'Darling... we all have... two deaths. First one, when our body... expires. Doesn't matter. Second death... permanent. That happens... when our name... is spoken for... the last time.'

I smiled at the towering river beast.

'Gorgo.'

TOKYO [SIDESHOW]

They wanted her bolted
   so good
     so calm   virtue-
shaped and gagged
to compress the muscles
of the mouth

but at her beautiful height
each defeated sound is edged
and shimmering
dread leaves the body
as silk made beetle
or bird –

the fiery ones with faces,
hands and feet that say
               all will be well
and

to speak through the wonderful
when no one else can understand
you, is a lesser kind of torture

BIG THINGS

The heart is massive
Pushes an ocean of life
The eyes see
And the brain feels
Thoughts bigger than your head

It is instinct to protect yourself against that which could wipe you
out
Simply by its steps around the world
Instinct to put a bullet in that giant head
And bring that giant body
Definitively down to your fragile Earth

(stop the monster stop the fear)

Instinct to look into those dying eyes
And see a universe
Fading
Under the startled glare of your confused eyes

Instinct to cry
Even though you are now safe
Instinct to feel
To sprout a tiny sympathy
For a dying giant

THE BEHAVIOUR OF BEARS

Haruo Nakajima
The man in the suit
Once spent a week at Tokyo's Ueno zoo
Where he studied the gait of elephants
And the behaviour of bears

He threw a piece of bread to the bears
To see how they would catch it
How would Gojira catch a plane?
A small object from the world of the big
Slamming into a giant fist in a celebration of relativity
How would He walk?
Ponderous and slow on a ground not meant for feet so big?
Our homes, our creative endpoints
Crushed like anthills
By an elephant's steps?

He once said:
'When elephants walk,
They never show the bottom of their feet.'

The suit weighed 100kg and took two people to put it on
Even then a person could only stay in it for three minutes at a time
'How can I act in this thing?' he asked himself.
A man who fought in a war
Who started his stunt career by setting himself on fire
Twelve times he would play Gojira and many other creatures besides
Stomping across the screen and in our imaginations

There is now an asteroid named after him stomping and
screaming through the universe
A celebration of Haruo Nakajima
The man in the suit
Catching planes in the zoo
Who never showed the bottom of his feet

ATTACK ROUTE FROM EAST RIVER

Wall street under foot when risen
    from oily waters barely concealing
a barnacled back of scale to think
    that none would be a slave to it.

Trading weapons lightly dusted
    by beaten mothwing choking up
the mechanisms of a gun barrel so
    cognisant of risk against the *ROI*

of flattened corporate sausage
    making factories. Arrogant bodies
in the district throw rolls of paper
    to curtail the rumbling of ancient

monsters as bribery, as cheapest
    deterrent to avoid the dismantling
of competitive modern office chair
    hierarchies. Without recompense

upon horizon, treading soil to write
    urban obituaries, a three headed
king comes again to reclaim what is
    rightfully ours as made by hand.

Recharge then these minority units.
    Scorch all battalions of lower to
middle tier management org charts
    and have them tremble at the depth

of massive imprints. The sheer
heat of radiation belched around
the serrations of gargantuan pointed
teeth readied to gnaw on each

laborious process is not enough.
To be sure all magnificent beasts
are unified in absolute destruction.
Rise up to save us from ourselves.

WHY I WANT TO FUCK GODZILLA

Even the first date institutes a revolutionary and practical new urbanism; our sheer romantic dynamism clearing the city of its privatised and over-policed spaces, its commercial and celebrity architecture, sky-pools, Millennium Domes, state-mandated quota art, speculative penthouses, palaces, police stations, Special Economic Zones, tax-free galleries; watch how we skip arm in titanic arm down Cannon Street, and third places sprout in our wake! Godzilla I believe is caring.

*

Any serious theorist of love will finally concede that it is precisely its furtive reclusion that makes it love: that the beloved qua loved is unknowable; but this needn't encourage a dogmatic irrationalism, a belief in symbols over facts, nor reduce the lover to a frantic hermeneuticist. All we need to love fully is a beloved at once entirely beyond us and, simultaneously, of entirely our own creation. We might call such a beloved *monster*, or 怪獣, *kaijū*, a Japanese jukugo or two-character compound of 怪, *kai*, 'suspicious,' 'mysterious,'; and 獣, *jū*, 'beast,' 'animal.' Every lover is a suspicious animal; every beloved a mysterious beast.

*

Godzilla was created by human beings. The claim of the 1954 film is that he was simply 'woken' by hydrogen bomb testing in the Pacific Ocean, but this ascription of the monster to some pre-existing, massive, and callously determinist Nature – *if* you bomb, *then* mindless Nature fights back – is a rationalisation or defanging of the more terrifying proposition: that human beings can indeed create objects so vast and powerful that they spiral entirely beyond our comprehension. Such objects are called *hyperobjects* by Timothy Morton. They are so big that they escape space, time, thought.

Why does Godzilla destroy Tokyo in 1954 and then, only ten years later, save the earth from King Ghidorah? We cannot understand. In fact we do not even attempt to. The mind shies from trying. A word for this shying is *love*.

*

Another human-made hyperobject is climate change. But one cannot fuck climate change.

*

Critics of communism will often accuse the movement of having essentially the same form as a religion: namely that it has adherents, sacred texts, prophets, schisms, heresies, frustrated apocalypses and so on. This might be true as far as it goes, which is not all that far. Much more significant, as John Berger says somewhere, is that communism is in part the belief that, through humankind's own productive activity, God will one day be dethroned and ourselves elevated to his place, whence to institute a Heaven on Earth. Perhaps forgotten is that a humankind so elevated will be, to the imprisoned human of the order of private property, a mysterious beast (怪獣, *kaijū*) of terrifying capabilities. At once human and God, which is to say: Jesus Christ.

*

King Ghidorah, it need hardly be said, is Satan. Milton:

> ... Him the Almighty Power
> Hurled headlong flaming from th'ethereal sky
> With hideous ruin and combustion
> Down to bottomless perdition, there to dwell ...

*

Newspaper headlines presented in the end credits of *Godzilla: King of the Monsters* (2019):

> 'Mysterious Rainforest Blooms in Sahara Desert'
> 'Godzilla's Path Through Pacific Bringing Life Back to Reefs, Restoring Fish Populations'
> ''Behemoth' Titan Restores Deforested Regions of Amazon'
> 'Scylla Slows Ice-Melt in Antarctica, Stabilizing Sea Levels'
> 'As Ecosystems Heal, 14 Species Taken Off Endangered Species List'
> 'Titan Waste Could Be Viable Energy Source'
> 'Massive Ancient Plants Resurface With Titans, Could Solve World Hunger Crisis'

It takes a hyperobject to defeat a hyperobject.

*

I am fond of *Godzilla: King of the Monsters*. I understand why it has detractors. Bradley Whitford's character – there can be no doubt – is extremely annoying. But even he must mutter, when the smoke and dust part on Godzilla's final victory over the satanic Ghidorah, and he is finally enthroned as the King of the Monsters – then even Bradley Whitford's execrable character must intone: *'Jesus.'*

*

King Kong is Adam. The two might ultimately be friends, but this is why Godzilla always wins.

*

In 1648, in *The Saint's Paradice*, the Digger Gerrard Winstanley – who advocated for the levelling of all hierarchy and the abolition of private property – described his vision of a material Heaven on Earth:

> And as all, and every one of them sees, enjoyes, and glories in the Father, so they see, enjoy and glory one in another, every one knowing, seeing, and sweetly rejoycing in the unity, and oneness of each others spirit; it being the spirit of the father, nay, the father himself, who is the spirit that fills all in all; and knits them together into one body, treading down all oppressing powers of the flesh forever, under their feet; and this is heaven in the largest sence, which every particular son and daughter of the father shall enjoy hereafter ...

Knit together into one body: the millenarian vision of communism is erotic. Donne, 'The Relic':

> First, we lov'd well and faithfully,
> Yet knew not what we lov'd, nor why;
> Difference of sex no more we knew
> Than our guardian angels do ...

Cf. Milton, 'Paradise Lost,' where the Archangel Raphael says to Adam:

> Whatever pure thou in the body enjoy'st
> (And pure thou wert created) we enjoy
> In eminence, and obstacle find none
> Of membrane, joynt, or limb, exclusive barrs:
> Easier than Air with Air, if Spirits embrace,
> Total they mix, Union of Pure with Pure
> Desiring; nor restrain'd conveyance need
> As Flesh to mix with Flesh, or Soul with Soul.

Communism is the practice by which we learn to fuck how angels fuck.

*

Godzilla Minus One is dimly aware of his erotic potential – hence its insistence on a thick, wide-hipped Godzilla. It ends with Godzilla penetrated, in the mouth, by our hero, who is encased within the metal body of a high-tech military aircraft. But this is not the joyful commingling of bodies that Godzilla-as-human-production promises for the communist utopia. It is rather the reconstitution of the ego of the warrior male, and, by extension, of the imperialist nation, both until then humiliated by defeat: this proto-fascist framework, for all its homely *Choose Life* messaging, cannot envision an erotic encounter that is not violent and does not tend toward extinction. Good movie though.

*

Against extinction, there are only three spheres of activity in which an individual human, the suspicious animal, can reach out to form bonds with the always-reclusive and mysterious beasts around them. One is the creation of art, the attempted transmission of secrets to secrets. One is the political project whose horizon is the secular Paradise of communism. The final is the various and multiple acts of love.

*

Godzilla is fictional. But I believe he would be a caring lover. Call it an article of faith.

HERE BE DRAGONS

My stomach was filigreed glass this morning.
This waiting, fizzing serpents from the abyss,
ever rising in their whispering,
And there was a woman on the telly
claiming water has memory,
And we are on the beach...

Canute, the water at his brow

And for the duration of this, for the sake of this poem,
we know more about the surface of the moon
than the ocean floor. Your lips are trembling
with fading words, as shivered aftershocks of myth
echo on the tip of a tongue, with everything important
stripped. For today, we are on the beach, as the unseen
falls in the deep, as the sea retreats at speed
before approaching Tsunami, stuck fast
in the quickening sands of memory,
And we are on the beach...

Canute, the water at his neck

Remembering that there is no agreed reason for deep-sea gigantism,
just theory and curiosity, and the limits of our technology,
Remembering there are no theoretical limits
to the size a beast can grow, as a heart slows
down, in the deep ocean,
How gigantism seethes where sunlight cannot reach

How we chase definition with folly, into the wine-dark sea,
Into the writhing fizzing serpents beneath,
And we are on the beach...

Canute, the water at his chest

And for the sake of internal logic, this water has memory,
for every tear must reach the sea, carrying its reason,
And somewhere, out there, giant serpents are feeding
upon our dreams. Scylla and Charybdis, Kraken and Leviathan,
swollen upon tragedies, *Adieu, adieu, adieu, Remember me*
Creeping diagnoses that wrap themselves around the world,
devouring our tales, growing malignant and fat upon our stories,
and distant memories, these insatiable beasts from the abyss,
Ouroboros, grown impossibly gigantic, an all-encompassing
Underpinning self-fulfilling prophecy...

Canute, the water at his knees

And we are on the beach, and I am stories enough
for both of us (or try to be), the sacrifice tied to the rock,
My stomach was hissing with snakes this morning,
And there was a woman on the telly claiming water has memory,
So, on the visit, I eat, and I feed, and I try to remember enough
for both of us, devouring tales to sustain us, bending myself
around a Mobius, telling your story so it echoes
on the tongue. And for the sake of this poem,
we are on the beach together,
telling tales, tall and sweet, of whispers over the horizon,
of the shifting unseen, far from home, where we know
a mind will eat itself, over and over,

Until it knows more about the surface of the moon,

than it does about the days of the week,

or the water at its feet,

as Jörmungandr eats.

And we are on the beach

as Jörmungandr eats.

Canute, the water at his toes

WORLD AS OTHER, WORLD AS BEAST
a response to Joanna Macy, after 'Godzilla: Planet of the Monsters'

It waited – that was the worst part.
For thousands of years without us, it grew

to be our armoured, insatiable fate.
Was it a '*wild love for the world*'

that invited this wildness? Was it love
that dragged its mountain through a sea of fire

towards the last survivors? Was that thread
of atomic breath – the one that pulled

the last evacuation ships out of the sky –
a cry at our departing back: '*don't leave,*

this is what we both want, it's better this way';
a roar to heaven from the burning earth

for us to go out, at the last, together?
It would wait – and if need be, forever.

DANCE TO AVERT THE APOCALYPSE
after 'Godzilla', 1954

Don't panic. This isn't the first time
that the fish have disappeared, that the sea
has boiled and spat monstrosity
upon us. We have had to climb

out of the wreckage. Centuries
of taking what we can has shown –
while appetites have only grown –
that we can see off threats like these.

Just pray what's coming feels the whirls
of long kimonos, hears the drum,
sees long-nosed masks, and will not come.
It's this, or we start sacrificing girls.

WE, HER MONSTERS

She gives fair warning. A gentle press of air that ripples overhead and sends you ducking for cover. Those of us who've been here longest are already under shelter, you get to know it's coming, like a storm when the air tightens. When the press of the clouds pushes on the crown of your head, and you can taste bitter orange in the yet to fall rain.

She enters the water slowly, She does everything slowly, too large to move fast. She is a glacial tear, not a landslide. In the water, She swims like an otter. Arms by Her side, legs by Her tail which drives Her through the depths.

She likes the water. You can sense that, too, under the scales in the pockets of air that get trapped there, the way it is in the feathers of a duck. She vibrates, a purr of contentment. I can understand it. Upright, on land, She's ponderous. Each step a colossal undertaking of bone and muscle. In the water She glides.

As She swims, She swallows shoals of fish. Pods of whale and dolphin. Later, when She surfaces, those of us chosen for the task will climb to Her mouth, pick the still flapping sea life from between Her teeth, and distribute it amongst the rest. Cooked on fires kindled from subcutaneous fat harvested as She sleeps. Kept stoked with shed keratin and driftwood, caught in the plates on Her back.

She is a bounty, a cornucopia, a generous leviathan. She can stand in one spot for so long, feet in the water, that Her shins become white with the guano of kittiwake. We descend on ropes amongst their screeching, whirling wings and collect their eggs.

Higher up, in the furnaces of Her throat, the forges work. Our smiths, their ears plugged to save themselves from going deaf, hammer scrap metal into pots and pans. The pink tinged blue of the flame turning even the most unyielding metal to rivers of gold. It is a pilot light that has never gone out, and though all who visit can smell the gasses in Her throat I've never seen it do any more than flicker.

At night we sleep under a green glow. The bioluminescence of the algae that grows in Her nooks. Though ignorant of whatever dark mechanisms keep Her going, we are warmed on the currents of Her blood.

We are Jonahs of convenience, and we only go skin deep.

I forget how long it has been like this. I think, sometimes, I remember Them coming. Though I would have been so small such a memory is impossible. I cannot remember Them waking from an age of sleep and breaking the world apart with Their yawning, stretching arms.

Spread imperfectly around the world, They emerged like bears from hibernation. Slow and hungry and clumsy with sleep. I don't think They meant to destroy as much as They did, I don't think They had a choice.

There are seven of Them. Each as large as the next, some with wings, some with great carapaces that harbour millions under Their shell. They have their preferred areas of habitation, each has Their own patch, but They're gentle creatures. If one meets another little more happens than would if a fox met another in a field. A little interest shown, then on. It's an opportunity for us, though. To jump ship if we want. Hooked ropes thrown from a back to a flank, the shimmy of emigrants each way. There are people here who have lived on all seven, some far older than I who remember the world before They woke, some who do not. Since my parents brought me aboard, when I was a child, I've never left. Why would I? Though I love to hear the stories of those who have, to hear about the places they've seen.

We are not the sum of us, of course. There are others who chose to hold on to civilisation when it fell. Mariners clinging to ships long since sunk. People who cannot, will not, let go of war and borders and property. Who would rather fight for scraps than share in a harvest. I'm told one still sits in the squashed circle of his office, in the debris of a broken dome and screams at the sky. Beats at his desk with little orange fists. What do they think, when we pass by?

Do they think they have won because She has forgotten them? As though She has noticed them at all. They are nothing, to Her. To any of Them.

This is not the first time They've woken. We're not the first She's carried. If you venture deeper in, into Her ears, Her nose, there are glyphs carved into Her flesh. Shards of pot and bone in long cold hearths. The brittle bones of early men. She's risen before, She'll sleep again. We'll learn nothing, or at least, what we learn will be forgotten. The wars will start again. The fires. I cannot decide if it is comforting or devastating, this proof of our cycles.

Perhaps They act as a reminder, proof, that under the right circumstances we can work together. That we can build and harvest just enough to live and be happy. But proof, too, that in the end we'll ask too much, that the ground and its blood and terror will call us with the promise of too much. I feel it. That when we leave, She'll sleep again. All of Them will. The ground will scab over, and scar, and new names will be found for the ridgelines and rivers that They leave in their wake. Until we get too loud and do it all over again.

I remember reading, in a book in the small, saved library, about parasites on the bodies of elephants. Remember the images of them, magnified to visibility. Their monstrous forms, alien shape. We are Her monsters. She carries us with Her. And we're grateful.

KISS CHASE

Come on!
Chase me down side streets
In shiny black helicopters
Bouncing bullet after bullet off of me

I topple buildings with the tip of my tail
Bite through your helicopter shell
And compose my poetry in the back of my mind
All the while

GROWLING NOISES

Grrr.

Grrrowr.

GrRRowl gr gr.

GrAAAAH! GRA-A-AAAH! Hrg. Gr-Hrgh Gr-HAAArgh.

If I bellow in the right way,

I can set the air alight.

Gr.

CITY PLANNING IN THE AGE OF MONSTERS

LIFE AS WE KNOW IT WILL SOON RESUME, CAN YOU
HEAR ME THROUGH THE ELEPHANTINE SHRIEK OF
LIMBS THICKER THAN THE LENGTH OF OUR DOCK
SCRAPING AGAINST STEEL, TECTONIC BACKS EELING
THE COAST TO A CHURN? THE BREEDING PROGRAM
HAS BEEN A GRAND SUCCESS. WE WILL SUBDUE THE
BEASTS ONCE THE SPIKE-TIPPED CEMENT MIXERS
FULL OF THORAZINE ARE READY; THEN PILE TONS
OF ROCK OVER THEM, AND IMPORTED SAND, DUNING
THEIR GREAT NECKS AND LATS; AND WE ARE LOOK-
ING FOR TWINS WHO ARE THE DAUGHTERS OF A TWIN
SO THEY CAN BE THE FIRST TO SET FOOT ON THE
ISLANDS, AND LIVE TO KEEP THE MONSTERS SLUMBER-
ING WITH SPELLS; BUT AT THE SAME TIME EQUALLY
SUMMONABLE WITH THE RIGHT RHYME IN BAHASA
SHOULD OUR NEIGHBOURS TRY ANYTHING. YOU KNOW
HOW IT IS; PEOPLE THESE DAYS WITH THEIR MONSTER
CULTURE, FEEDING SMOG TO ROGUE HEDORAHS AND
EATING GENETICALLY MODIFIED BIOLLANTE FRUIT
AND FLYING F16S IN TRIDENT-FORMATION WITH THEIR
GHIDORAHS. BUT DON'T WORRY; WE ARE BEGINNING
TO INSTALL DEFENSIVE EGGS UNDER THE STREETS,
AS A FORWARD-THINKING MEASURE. SOME MEASURES
ARE NECESSARY IN SUCH A TERRIBLE WORLD. THIS
LIFE OF NORMAL AND ALWAYS THE SAME.

ANAGRAMMATIC KAIJU BLUES
after Yeow Kai Chye

'And then we found out that the Precursors [who released the Kaiju]
are us thousands of years in the future,' he continued. 'They're trying
to terraform, trying to re-harvest the earth to survive.'
— Guillermo Del Toro, on his nixed plans for Pacific Rim 2

looming above the tallest tower,	*gall heat retools bone-wove mitt*
bigger than everything you love	*hit glob vigour they've an energy*
and then some; broken vows, turned	*Tom's kerned tow-van shone, burned*
silicate and cyan. future gloved	*a cuter silly cove fund. I ate, dang*
in rotting meat. when you punch through us,	*he that tough guise, runt prion. munchy now.*
you find more *you*; thrusting, deadly, back.	*yon fiery rust-backed mouth, dying aloud*

your youngest selves oozing black fluids,

sunday sling fool bucks elver zygotes, oui,

arms cannon-tipped, demanding evac.

snip, decant dam. conga dive per man.

still, grace, in our webbed wings' giant arcs,

I slit gore beadings, a cursing bract we win

the eggs lighting our flowerlike maws.

weak gull legs wither if ghosting Rome.

we are the last shark's eyes going dark,

gone East. the gars leak. yes, ward, shirk

the kind of warning you cannot ignore.

wet, caring round; oh; finning, oaky note

WAIST-HIGH IN THE WORLD
after Nancy Mairs

Most comfortable walking half in water, I
slake the bay's cranes with my waddle –
all hip knob and gangle, city's eclipse.
As the droplets I shake free of my hair
crater hastily vacated cars – spike skyline –
I wait for the crew to douse me
before the rubber sparks
squib! Breathless with blast

I tug at the wires in my hips,
falling half out of this rubbery shell –
a torso dropped to damp deflation.
Turn the knobs, spin the platform's ganglia!
I rig a craned exit – with the right wheelie,
        I might almost fly!
Thus installed, I wheel to life's next great soundstage –
a crater in rain, my city sparking just above the lip.

William Steffen is an associate professor of English at American International College in Springfield, Massachusetts, where he teaches courses on Shakespeare, creative writing, and feminist horror films. His scholarship focuses on the environmental humanities and the English stage, and he is the author of *Anthropocene Theater and the Shakespearean Stage*. His creative writing has been featured in *Full Bleed, Last Girls Club, Deal Jam Magazine,* and *Empyrean Literary Magazine.* He lives in Holyoke, MA, with his wife and two children.

James Sullivan is the author of *Harboring* (ELJ Editions), a literary interpretation of the Japanese ‹Giant Hero› genre. His stories and essays have appeared in *Cimarron Review*, *New Ohio Review*, *Third Coast*, *Fourth Genre*, *The Normal School*, and *Fourteen Hills* among other publications. In 2022, he was a finalist for the Tobias Wolff Award for Fiction, but he still thinks often of *Bambi vs Godzilla*. Connect on The Legion (X) @ jfsullivan4th.

A Creative Writing MFA graduate from Oklahoma State University, **Wyeth Leslie** (he/him) is a humanist poet and writer interested in pop culture, technology, and beautiful mundane lives. He is the author of the sci-fi hued poetry collection, *This Machine Keeps the Ghost*, from Alien Buddha Press. Other writings have been featured in publications such as Drunk Monkeys, Bridge Eight Press, Film Cred, The Daily Drunk, and Haywire Magazine. He can be found on Letterboxd and the site formerly known as Twitter.

David Spittle is a poet, filmmaker and essayist. He is the author of four collections of poetry (*All Particles and Waves*, *Rubbles*, *Decomposing Robert*, *How Eyes Rest*) and the pamphlet, *BOX*. His short films have been screened internationally and his book of interviews, *Light Glyphs*, celebrates poets talking about film and filmmakers talking about poetry.

Dr. Amy Gaeta is a scholar, poet, and disability justice advocate. They are a Research Associate at the Leverhulme Centre for the Future of Intelligence at the University of Cambridge. They use feminist disability studies to analyze the emotional, aesthetic, and political dimensions of human-tech relations. In poetry, They examine mental illness, desire, and the impossibility of 'the human.' They have published two poetry chapbooks, *The Andy Poems* (Red Mare Press, 2021), and *Prosthetics & Other Organs (*Dancing Girl Press, 2023).

Daisy Edwards (she/her) is an autistic, bisexual writer born and raised in Lancashire, currently living in Birmingham. Last year she was nominated for the Pushcart Prize by Arboreal Literary Magazine and her work has featured in Written Off Publishing, Sunday Mornings at the River, Spelt Magazine, and Rotted Magazine. This year, her poetry will be in the York Literary Review, Lucent Dreaming's For A Friend Anthology, and Vocivia Magazine. Follow her on Instagram @dredwards_writes

Atlas Weyland Eden is an 18-year-old writer and poet, living on the edge of Dartmoor. He started his first novel at the age of nine, and hasn't looked back since. When he was 13, his story 'Satan & Pan' won Chagword's Short Story Competition. Since then he's won various writing awards, including the Young Walter Scott Prize and the BBC Young Writers' Award. He loves stories of nature and folklore, particularly Japanese culture and myth.

Bex Hainsworth is a poet and teacher based in Leicester, UK. She won the Collection HQ Prize as part of the East Riding Festival of Words and has been shortlisted in the Welsh Poetry Competition, Waltham Forest Poetry Competition, and the AUB International Poetry Prize. Her work has appeared in Atrium, Ink Sweat & Tears, Honest Ulsterman, and bath magg. *Walrussey*, her debut pamphlet of ecopoetry, is published by The Black Cat Poetry Press.

George K. Angelou is an aspiring author of speculative fiction. The Thing I Am is George's first published story in the genre, and he's currently putting the finishing touches on his first science fiction novel. George also runs the YouTube channel Write Like a Legend, where he analyses the literary techniques used by his favorite authors, and shares his thoughts on writing theory.

David Thompson is a poet from Droitwich Spa, Worcestershire. His work has featured in magazines and anthologies including *Atrium, Dream Catcher, Magma* and *Under the Radar*.

Jon Stone is a Derbyshire-born writer, researcher and editor who specialises in hybrid, ludic and collaborative literary forms. His recent publications are *Unravelanche* (Broken Sleep, 2021), *Sandsnarl* (The Emma Press, 2021) and *Dual Wield: The Interplay of Poetry and Video Games* (DeGruyter, 2022). He edits and publishes multi-author mixed-genre anthologies with Sidekick Books, and teaches at Anglia Ruskin University. His website is www.gojonstonego.com

Jen Farr is the editor of *Idle Ink*, an online publisher of all things curious. Her stories have been published in *The Chamber Magazine, The Daily Drunk, STORGY,* and others. She owns more books than she could ever possibly read and doesn't get out much. To read more of her work, visit www.jenfarr.co.uk or follow her on Instagram @jen_farr_is_here.

Nic Stringer is a writer who also works with visual and sound material. *Hemispheres* is available at Guillemot Press, and her first collection, *A day that you happen to know* was highly commended in the Forward Prizes 2018. More at corruptedpoetry.com

Colin Harris-Day is a poet and hospitality drone based in Merseyside. His most recent book is *The Poet's Cane* from Alien Buddha Press. Prior to this anthology his only connection to kaiju was his time in a failed guitar band called Kiwi Gojira at the age of sixteen. Fortunately, he writes better than he plays guitar.

Stuart McPherson is a prize-winning poet from the UK. His poems have appeared in Butcher's Dog Magazine, Bath Magg, Poetry Wales, Anthropocene, Blackbox Manifold, Finished Creatures, and The87press. In October 2022, Stuart was the winner of the Ambit Annual Poetry Competition. His second collection 'End Ceremonies' was published via Broken Sleep Books on August 31st 2023.

Patrick Ball is a teacher and a writer of poetry and fiction from Sheffield, currently living in London. Before that he taught English in Kyoto, Japan, and studied philosophy in Philadelphia, USA.

Rick Dove is a progressive poet and activist from South London. Published in anthologies, zines, and journals since 2016, Rick also has two solo collections with Burning Eye Books; *Tales From the Other Box* (2020), *Supervillain Origin Story* (2023) and was crowned UK Poetry Slam Champion in 2021.

Tim Kiely is a criminal barrister and writer based in East London. His poetry has been published in a number of outlets including *South Bank Poetry, Ink, Sweat & Tears, Under the Radar* and *Magma.* He is the author of three poetry pamphlets: *Hymn to the Smoke* (a winner of the 2020 Indigo Dreams First Pamphlet Competition); *Plaque for the Unknown Socialist*; and *No Other Life* (a winner of the 2023 Brian Dempsey Memorial Competition). Buy his books at timkielybooks.bigcartel.com

Sam K. Horton lives above the moor in Cornwall. After training as a costume designer, then working as an artist he turned to writing, finding to his frustration and delight that he liked it better than drawing and should have been doing it all along. His debut novel, *Gorse*, comes out in September 2024 from Solaris, with a sequel to follow. He is represented by John Baker and Julie Gourinchas at Bell, Lomax, Morton.

Wes Viola is a pen-name of Wes White, who is an Elder Bard of Glastonbury and a past winner for poetry at Wells Festival of Literature. His work has featured recently in Obsessed With Pipework, Eunoia Review, Bog, Dreich, Visual Verse, and Trash Wonderland; as well as Broken Sleep's 'Masculinity' anthology earlier this year.

Jack Xi (they/he) is a goat-headed fish-tailed giant sometimes ensconced within an alien throne called a 'wheelchair'. They've appeared in several poetry journals, anthologies, and coastal city warning alerts. Find out more at jackxisg.wordpress.com

CRUSH YOUR UNREST